Code

Context Architecture: Fundamental Concepts Between Art, Science, and Technology

Digitalization has altered architectural discourse. Today, discussions in architectural theory and design are shaped by many new ideas, including some that previously had no meaning in that context, or else very different ones. Increasingly, the conceptualizations and strategies of architectural discourse are molded by influences emerging along the interface joining scientific and cultural images of modern information technology. Posing itself against this background is the question: on the basis of which practical and in particular which theoretical concepts can architecture come to terms with these new technologies, thereby entering into a simultaneously productive and critical dialog with them? Presented for debate in *Context Architecture* is a selection of such ideas, all of them central to current discourses. *Context Architecture* is a collaboration of the Zurich University of the Arts (ZHdK) and the Ludger Hovestadt, chair for Computer Aided Architectural Design at the ETH Zurich.

Also available in the series Context Architecture:

Simulation. Presentation Technique and Cognitive Method
ISBN 978-3-7643-8686-3

Complexity. Design Strategy and World View
ISBN 978-3-7643-8688-7

Pattern. Ornament, Structure, and Behavior
ISBN 978-3-7643-8954-3

Code. Between Operation and Narration
ISBN 978-3-0346-0117-7

Context Architecture
A collaboration of the Zurich University of the Arts (ZHdK) and the ETH Zurich

Z

Zürcher Hochschule der Künste
Zurich University of the Arts

CAAD Professur Hovestadt
ETH Zürich

Code

Between Operation and Narration

CONTEXT ARCHITECTURE

Edited by Andrea Gleiniger and Georg Vrachliotis

Birkhäuser
Basel

Translation from German into English: Laura Bruce, Berlin
Project management: Karoline Mueller-Stahl, Leipzig

Cover and layout design: Bringolf Irion Vögeli GmbH, Zurich
Reproductions and typesetting: weissRaum visuelle Gestaltung, Basel

This book is also available in German: *Code. Zwischen Operation und Narration*
ISBN 978-3-0346-0116-0.

Library of Congress Control Number: 2010923974

Bibliographic information published by the German National Library
The German National Library lists this publication in the Deutsche Nationalbibliografie; detailed bibliographic data are available on the Internet at http://dnb.d-nb.de.

Basel
P.O. Box 133, CH-4010 Basel, Switzerland

Printed on acid-free paper produced from chlorine-free pulp. TCF ∞

Printed in Germany

ISBN 978-3-0346-0117-7

9 8 7 6 5 4 3 2 1

www.birkhauser-architecture.com

EDITORIAL

The philosopher Friedrich Kittler gave a lecture at *Ars Electronica 2003* entitled "Code oder wie sich etwas anders schreiben lässt" (Code – or How to Write Something in a Different Way).[1] The lecture focused on the code theory's fundamental significance, which is increasingly overshadowed by the dominance of techno-scientific fields of research. Codes are not simply a "peculiarity of computer technology or gene technology" – as is often assumed. They far more belong "to all communications and transmission media."[2] Kittler's lecture approached the code theory from a conceptual historical perspective, but more importantly, he sensitized his listeners then and his readers now to the complex spectrum of meaning of an abstract concept oscillating between the technical and the cultural in a very specific way.

In the mid-twentieth century and, thus, in the shadow of the onset of the computer sciences, a semiotic discourse formed around the philosopher Max Bense, which was strongly influenced by Norbert Wiener's *Cybernetics* and Claude Shannon's mathematical theory of communication, called the *information theory.* This discourse focused on the concepts of "sign," "language," "code," as well as of "aesthetics." Studying computer codes became an artistic field of experimentation, rather than purely a means to serve mathematical processes. The places that accommodated computers began to change into interdisciplinary laboratories where artists, musicians, and architects would gather, despite the fact that – and this was a highly unique situation at the time – it was mathematicians, such as Frieder Nake and Georg Nees, who initially claimed to embody a new type of artist. In line with Kittler, the computer graphics they created by means of random generators can be interpreted as the aesthetic residue of "technical writing."[3]

Architecture would be rediscovered as a *"Bedeutungsträger"* (carrier of meaning) shortly thereafter, in response to the efforts at reduction made by functionalism and international style, and significantly influenced by Robert

1 Friedrich Kittler, "Code oder wie sich etwas anders schreiben lässt," Lecture at the *Ars Electronica,* Linz, September 6–11, 2003. Printed in the exhibition catalog *Code. The Language of our Time,* ed. by Gerfried Stocker and Christine Schöpf, Linz, 2003, pp. 15–19, here: p. 15.

2 Ibid.

3 See Friedrich Kittler, *Draculas Vermächtnis. Technische Schriften,* Leipzig, 1993.

Venturi and Denise Scott Brown. In postmodern architectural discourses, the concept of code – particularly under the influence of semiotics – was used as a semantic category. The question of form became a question of meaning. The concept of code endowed architecture with fresh cultural polysemy.

In 1987, Peter Eisenman adapted the code theory as a biological metaphor for an architectural concept in his design for the Institute of Biochemistry in Frankfurt. Eisenman continues to make efforts to associate the various aspects of meaning that underlie coding (and codification). As, for example, in his City of Culture of Galicia for Santiago de Compostela, where he refers to the religious traditions of the *codici* in terms of a system that generates a world view, or when he operates and experiments with an instrumentarium of information technology as a means of design strategy.[4]

In contrast, the notion of code today is more ubiquitous than ever in its operationalizing function as a computer code – and this applies particularly to architectural strategies, which are increasingly defined by algorithms.[5] At the same time the concept of code begins to clearly oscillate between the two architectural poles of function and meaning. The question concerning the actual significance of this development formed the basis for our research into the code's diverse, architecture-related conceptual fields of gravitation.

The essay by architectural theorist *Claus Dreyer* provides an overview of the spectrum and historical development of "design codes" that have become the foundation of primarily postmodern architectural theory, but in particular that of Charles Jencks. This code theory, which is strongly influenced by semiotics, can be used to describe the heterogeneous field of the contemporary architectural design conventions to which various cultural practices adhere, and which are, hence, seldom strictly codified. Dreyer traced the most important stations of the concept of code's application in a semiotic-oriented architectural discourse. He goes on to explain how new codes are generated by developments in technology, society, and science, and how they become the expression of recent history's plural concept of the world and of ourselves, as well as of the cultural sensitivities of today. This type of discussion, concerning

4 See Cynthia Davidson (ed.), *Code X. The City of Culture of Galicia*, New York, 2005; Luca Galofaro (ed.), *Digital Eisenman. An Office of the Electronic Era*, Basel, Boston, Berlin, 1999.

5 See Kostas Terzidis, *Algorithmic Architecture*, Amsterdam, 2006.

the concept of code and its various forms, sheds light on an abstract concept that has been presented for fundamental negotiation and discussion repeatedly since the beginning of the nineteenth century: the concept of style. The subject has never actually been entirely omitted from the architectural theoretical discourse. It was, however, always exposed to a similar fundamental challenge and the associated, conceptually weakened form, as experienced by the ornamental theory. *Andrea Gleiniger* analyzes the relationship between the concept of code and style in her essay. If the focus here lies in the extent to which the code theory has attempted to replace the style concept, then one must examine the various forms of defining validity that the two concepts developed and are developing, as well as the type of discourses in which this validity had and still has to be verified. An informative context is provided by the paradigmatic shift to which, today, an architecture-related code theory in the contradictory field of semantic meaning and algorithmic function is subjected. Postmodernism programmatically linked "code" to the function of narrative, meaning theories of fictionalization in which histories and stories, as contextualizing references, could be designed architecturally and put very consciously into practice.

Compared with the more static concept of fiction, the concept of narration reveals the system behind the narration process, which materializes architecturally by means of influences rather than pictures. The philosopher *Gabriele Gramelsberger* pursues these new qualities of narration. Her essay considers the topic of how the computer code spawns ever-new ways of narrating about nature, environment, technology, and architecture. "Story Telling with Code," as Gramelsberger calls this type of narration, sheds new light not only on the idea of narration, but also on that of digital architectural production. However, is not a new method of interpretation also needed to accompany the new concept of story telling, perhaps even a fundamentally new understanding of how architecture can be perceived and designed? She critically poses the question as to whether an omnipresence might not be attributed to the computer code and, thus, to the (de)mythologizing consequences of programming. It is certainly true, as the computer scientist *Georg Trogemann* diagnoses in his essay, that computer programs have long advanced to become indispensable assistants that play essential roles in producing new knowledge and methods, such as inventing new materials, serving as complex substantiation in mathematics, or when simulating weather conditions. Trogemann studies the underlying problem of how the code managed to become this all-pervading, and which hidden impact it may have on the results of our work processes, and, hence, on architectural practice.

A quick look back at the almost 50-year-long history of architecture and the computer will show that, at the beginning of the 1960s, the computer was still unchartered technological territory for architects, and considered primarily an artifact by technicians for technicians. It opened to architects a still foreign world of codes and programs that was also appealing, because they were fascinated by the mysterious and alluring glamor of technology. Now, with this in mind, the question then emerged of how this new machine can be operated and used in the design process. *Georg Vrachliotis* assumes that this question, in respect to architecture, also points to a certain historicity. He shows that the apparently simple matter, of how the computer can be used in architecture, contains not only two different postwar era discourses, but also two fundamentally different cultural philosophies of architecture, art, and technology.

In view of Kittler's above-quoted reference to the diversity of meaning, and Eisenman's attempt to relate different aspects of the code theory, it becomes clear that the essential question of the definition of a code will always involve its metaphoric imagery. The philosopher Hans Blumenberg reflected in depth on the role and the specific function of metaphors as being "for the opening and the understanding of the world and as a constitutive element of thought."[6] In his *Paradigms for a Metaphorology,* published in 1960, Blumenberg reflects on this same topic within the framework of a conceptual history of philosophy. He is interested in the metaphors of *philosophical* language. But comparable questions can also be formed in relation to the language of other disciplines. For example, when the philosopher *Karim Bschir* questions the use of metaphors in science, such as in the science of molecular biology where the concept of code is uniquely appropriated to serve the "genetic code." Bschir discusses two perspectives of this question in his essay. The first begins with the assumption that we use metaphors "wherever our vocabulary is not yet

6 See Hans Blumenberg, *Paradigms for a Metaphorology,* transl. with an afterword by Robert Savage, Ithaca (forthcoming in 2010) (German original edition 1960).

mature enough to formulate all our knowledge in a positive and strictly rational manner"; in this example, metaphors function as linguistic tools. The second perspective postulates, with a reference to Blumenberg, that metaphors are the "basic elements of language" and have their own expressive function and generate their own meanings. We believe that the second perspective is particularly productive from an architectural theory point of view. Accordingly, one of architectural theory's core tasks could be to constantly work on identifying and clarifying the conceptual history, as well as on the critical revision and contextualization, of the metaphor's function as generator of meaning.

We thank the authors for their well informed essays, which were prepared specifically for this book. Moreover, this volume of the *Context Architecture* series could not have been realized in content or form without the generous support of the Zurich University of the Arts and its founding director Hans-Peter Schwarz, and Ludger Hovestadt, Chair for Computer Aided Architectural Design (CAAD) at the ETH Zurich, to whom we are sincerely grateful. It is also obvious that a project such as this is unthinkable without the support of an expert and well-informed editor. Karoline Mueller-Stahl's participation was marked by competence, patience, and commitment. We are also thankful to Robert Steiger, Senior Editor of the architecture department, for taking on the project in Birkhäuser Verlag. We hope to have the opportunity to continue this productive collaboration, which represents a dialog between architecture, art, science, and technology, but also the transdisciplinary aspirations of two institutions.

Andrea Gleiniger & Georg Vrachliotis

Karim Bschir

TRANSIENT OR FUNDAMENTAL? THE CODE METAPHOR IN MOLECULAR BIOLOGY

It is difficult to actually define the term "code," considering the vast number of different codes that exist. There is the Morse code, for example, and there are codes for computer programs. We use PIN codes to protect our credit cards, and entry codes to access our email accounts, there are social codes, and activation codes for nuclear weapons. And, for the last fifty years or so, there has been yet another very special code: the genetic code.

The term "genetic code" designates the key mechanism by which the cells of biological organisms translate a sequence of nucleotides into a sequence of amino acids. The genetic code assigns each possible triplet out of the four bases – adenine, thymine, cytosine, and guanine – to one of the 20 amino acids that build up proteins. In short, during protein synthesis, a long chain of nucleic acid bases (the basic components of DNA) is translated into a long chain of amino acids (the basic components of proteins), and the genetic code provides the rules for this translation.

Today we are convinced that the blueprint for nearly all forms of life is, in the language of the genetic code, inscribed on the DNA molecule and that genetic information determines many characteristics of each individual. What is more, this belief is no longer just a part of a specialized *scientific* knowledge, but it actually molds our general understanding of mankind. One could even say that the genetic code is now accepted as *the* paradigm of a code. This is, indeed, a remarkable fact, because the genetic code does not possess the characteristics which are normally associated with a code. We generally understand a code as something that someone has invented in order to codify information or to protect it from unauthorized access. The codified transmission of information generally arises from the context of human *intent* and *purpose.* Usually, it is the contents and the meaning of the codified information which are considered worth protecting. This raises some interesting questions regarding the genetic code: Who invented the genetic code? Is it an encryption? And, if so, for whom? What precisely is the meaning of genetic information? Must the relationship between DNA and protein be understood as a semantic one at all?

It is of course quite legitimate to call the relationship between the base sequence of DNA and the amino acid sequence of a protein a code. Yet from another point of view, this particular code apparently lacks some of the characteristics normally identified in a code. Hence, it is often claimed that the terms "genetic code" or "genetic information" are, in effect, pure metaphors.

If these terms are actually only mere metaphors, then one would expect that they can be more widely found in the popular press and, hence, that at the forefront of biological research a less metaphorical vocabulary is employed. But this is not at all the case. Expressions such as "genetic information," "genetic code," "codon," "sense strand," "translation," "transcription," "palindrome," "genomic library" or "open reading frame," are all established terminology in molecular biology.[1] In fact, it seems as though modern biological vocabulary can hardly be thought of without the large number of metaphors that were once borrowed from other scientific disciplines like linguistics and information science. This essay aims to shed light on how those terms made their way into the field of biology, and how the transfer of terms from one scientific discipline to another – in this case from mathematical information science to biology – led to an innovative research program and to the development of an independent vocabulary that is still very much used today, even after the full sequencing of the human genome.[2]

The history of this began in the 1940s. In 1948, Claude Shannon published his *Mathematical Theory of Communication* and thereby founded "information theory," the predecessor of computer science.[3] One notable aspect of Shannon's theory was that it conceived of "information" as purely quantitative.

1 For further information see: Jeremy M. Berg, John L. Tymoczko, and Lubert Stryer, *Biochemistry,* 6th ed., New York, 2006.

2 The story of this transition has been excellently told by Lily Kay, and Kay can be consulted on much of what follows. For example, she writes: "In that postwar world order, the material, discursive, and social practices of molecular biology were transformed. Information theory, cybernetics, systems analyses, electronic computers, and simulation technologies fundamentally altered the representations of animate and inanimate phenomena. [...] It is within this information discourse that the genetic code was constituted as an object of study and a scriptural technology, and the genome textualized as a latter-day Book of Life." Lily E. Kay, *Who Wrote the Book of Life. A History of the Genetic Code,* Stanford, 2000, p. 5.

3 Claude E. Shannon, "The Mathematical Theory of Communication," in *Bell System Technical Journal* 27 (1948), pp. 379–423 and pp. 623–656. Shannon's work was published incidentally in the same year Norbert Wiener published his *Cybernetics* (Norbert Wiener, *Cybernetics. Or Communication and*

Within the context of the theory, "information" was understood exclusively as the amount of information contained within a character or a string of characters. The degree of information of a certain character correlates logarithmically with the statistical probability of its occurrence. The more frequently a character occurs, the smaller the quantity of its information is, and vice versa. The semantic dimension, in other words, that which a character represents, its meaning, plays absolutely no role in Shannon's theory. Shannon's information theory treats information as a purely statistical factor. This makes his approach differ greatly from other theories of information and also from common notions of it.

Shannon developed his theory in the *Bell Telephone Laboratories,* an industrial research institute that was dedicated to developing new applications in electronics, physics, chemistry, radio technology, and mathematics. Shannon's mathematical model, that is, the statistical quantification and the associated "de-semanticizing" of the concept of information, were unmistakably serving *Bell Labs'* application-oriented research; and the theory itself surely owes some of its success to this pragmatic association with concrete technical research interests. With the advent of information theory, the foundations were laid for a broad and extremely multi-applicable research practice in the fields of communication technology, cryptology, and information processing. Its success led to establishing an independent, information-theoretical vocabulary with some powerful topoi which could easily be employed in other scientific disciplines. One of those was the topos of "code."

The first use of the code metaphor to describe biological processes can be traced back to a small book with a wonderful title: *What Is Life?,* written by physicist Erwin Schrödinger. In it, Schrödinger examines genetic heredity and dedicates a chapter to "the hereditary mechanism." He writes, "it is these chromosomes [...] that contain in some kind of code-script the entire pattern of the individual's future development and of its functioning in the mature state. Every complete set of chromosomes contains the full code [...] In calling the

Control in the Animal and the Machine, Cambridge/Mass., 1948). Although Shannon and Wiener worked independently of one another, there are obvious parallels in their research. It is highly possible that Wiener, as professor of mathematics at the Massachusetts Institute of Technology, had significant influence on Shannon as he did his PhD at MIT. See footnote 2, p. 93.

structure of the chromosome fibres a code-script we mean that the all-penetrating mind, once conceived by Laplace, to which every causal connection lay immediately open, could tell from their structure whether the egg would develop, under suitable conditions, into a black cock or into a speckled hen into a fly or a maize plant, a rhododendron, a beetle, a mouse or a woman."[4]

This vividly illustrates the conceptual transition that took place in biology in the first half of the twentieth century. Ever since the advent of modern biology in the nineteenth century, the classification of organisms and the study of their phenotypical structures were the main interests of biologists. Since the living was distinguishable from the nonliving by its high degree of organization, the primary aim of biology was to understand biological organization phenomena. To this organization discourse, the concept of specificity was central. It was assumed that there are genuinely biological factors which determine the specific phenotypical characteristics of an organism. Gregor Mendel discovered in his hybridization experiments that certain phenotypical characteristics were passed on to progeny according to particular laws and with a high level of regularity.[5] The question arose of how, over many generations, nature was able to maintain such a high level of specificity and organization for such highly differentiated structures. Charles Darwin himself found particular interest in the questions of this maintenance of specificity too. According to Darwin, a credible theory of heredity would have to explain how the specific organic structures of different life forms were passed on from generation to generation.

However, the lack of a good theory of heredity at the time led Darwin to develop his own extremely interesting and innovative, even though highly speculative, "theory of pangenesis."[6] So the central questions in late nineteenth century's biology were: How is specificity maintained, how are characteristics passed on, and how is it possible for a particular phenotypical structure to reproduce itself? In 1894, the German chemist Hermann Emil Fischer formu-

4 Erwin Schrödinger, *What Is Life? The Physical Aspect of the Living Cell,* Cambridge/UK, 1944.

5 Gregor Johann Mendel, *Experiments in Plant Hybridization* (paper presented at the Natural History Society of Brünn meetings of February 8th and March 8th, 1865).

6 Charles Darwin, *Variation of Animals and Plants under Domestication,* 2nd ed., London, 1883, chap. 27. See also: Eva Jablonka and Marion J. Lamb, *Evolution in Four Dimensions. Genetic, Epigenetic, Behavioral, and Symbolic Variation in the History of Life,* Cambridge/Mass., 2006, chap. 1.

lated the so-called "lock-and-key hypothesis," which describes the binding specificity between an enzyme and its substrate, so that the question of specificity subsequently found a correspondence not only on the phenomenal, organic, but also on the molecular level: How can an enzyme bind to a substrate with such high specificity and, thereby, catalyze a very particular chemical reaction?

The question of specificity is still present in Schrödinger: How can a chicken, again, produce a chicken, a fly a fly, a maize plant a maize plant etc.? However, what makes Schrödinger's quote so enlightening is not so much its tie to the specificity problem of the late nineteenth century, but rather that it contains a conceptual shift from addressing the question of specificity towards addressing, instead, the means by which biological *information* is transferred.[7] This semantic shift appears in the quote above where Schrödinger explicitly speaks of some kind of "code script" which might contain all of the necessary "information" on a single chromosome.

Even though the terms "specificity" and "information" are both excellently suited for describing the complex organization of biological structures, they nonetheless bear an important difference in their connotation, which can be described as follows: The term "specificity" always points towards the Aristotelian material cause, that which explains *what from,* from which *matter,* a thing grows, i.e. a fly from a fly, a chicken from a chicken, and so on. Darwin also conceived "inheritance" as a phenomenon of growth, by which progeny grows from small, particles (which he called "gemmules") in the bodies of the parents.[8] In contrast to this, the term "information" addresses the Aristotelian formal cause, that is the non-material factor that determines something material to become the particular thing it is. According to the Aristotelian view all material structures must be *in-formed.* The essence of a certain material structure is established not until matter gets its form.[9]

7 The hypothesis that "information" replaced biological "specificity" was formulated by Kay: "My thesis is that molecular biologists used 'information' as a metaphor for biological specificity." Kay, see footnote 2, p. 2.

8 "Inheritance must be looked at as merely a form of growth." With this sentence, Darwin summarized the essence of his own theory. See Darwin, footnote 6, p. 398.

9 Referring to Aristotle at this stage is not at all a farfetched anachronism. The scientists involved in deciphering the genetic code also understood their project as a search for the form factors that determine organisms. Max Delbrück, who was awarded the Nobel Prize in 1969 together with

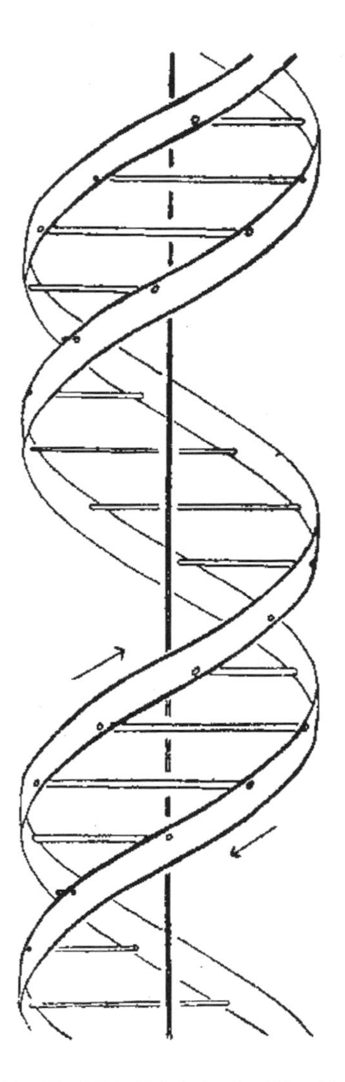

Fig. 1: The schematic presentation of the DNA double helix from the 1953 article by Watson and Crick.

Yet when biological "information" is understood as a formal factor, then this particular terminology presupposes the existence of some type of material template that would store the information. Schrödinger was obviously aware of this. Although he did not yet know the chemical properties of DNA, it was obvious for him to assume that chromosomes were the most likely candidate for a carrier of biological information. In the very same year in which Schrödinger published *What Is Life?,* Oswald Avery discovered that it actually is the nucleic acid fraction of a cell – and not the proteins as had previously been assumed – that carries genetic information.[10]

A few years later James Watson and Francis Crick resolved the three-dimensional, double-helical structure of the DNA molecule using X-ray crystallography[11] [Fig. 1]. The identification of nucleic acids as a storage system for genetic information, the resolution of their structure in addition to Schrödinger's inspiration of conceiving the transfer of information as a code with a linear sequence and a small number of units, these were the decisive factors that caused an awareness for a highly fascinating scientific project yet to come: the deciphering of the genetic code.

One scientist who was particularly fascinated by the idea that the newly discovered DNA might possibly contain a code, which had to be deciphered like the code of a foreign secret service, was the physicist George Gamow, a Russian in American exile who was also one of the founding fathers of Big Bang Theory. Gamow, together with Francis Crick and James Watson, organized the so-called "RNA Tie Club." This club of scientists (at meetings, they all wore ties with the double helix pattern) took on the task of "cracking the RNA amino acid

Salvador Luria and Alfred Hershey for his research on bacteriophages, once told his audience during a lecture a serious joke. He pointed out to the Nobel Prize Committee that is was actually Aristotle who first suggested the formal principle of DNA, and that the committee should consider Aristotle when awarding the prize next time. See Max Delbrück: "Aristotle-totle-totle," in *Of Microbes and Life,* ed. by Jacques Monod and Ernest Borek, New York, 1971.

10 See Oswald T. Avery, Colin M. MacLeod, and Maclyn McCarty, "Studies on the Chemical Nature of the Substance Inducing Transformation of Pneumococcal Types," in *Journal of Experimental Medicine* 79 (February 1944), pp. 137–158.

11 James D. Watson and Francis H. C. Crick, "Molecular Structure of Nucleic Acids," in *Nature* 171 (April 1953), pp. 737–738.

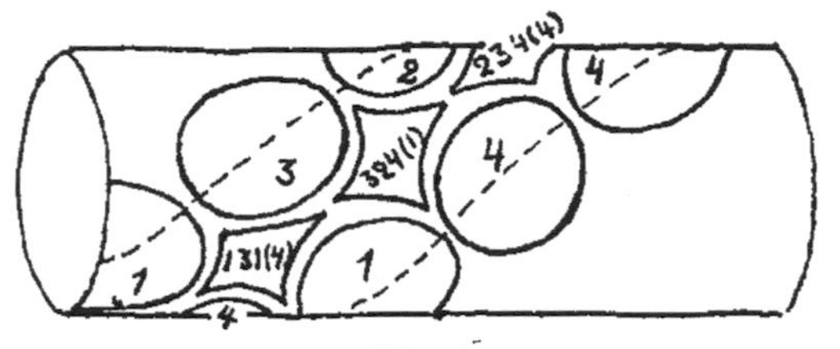

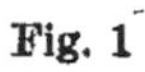

Fig. 1

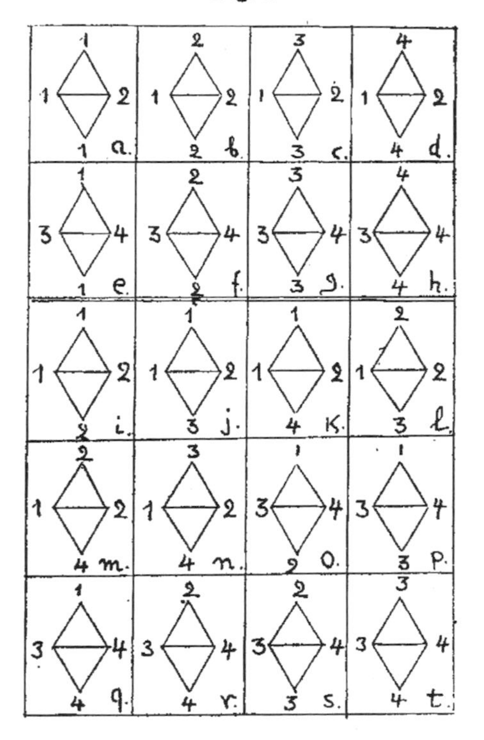

Fig. 2: Gamow's "diamond code." George Gamow: "Possible Relation between Deoxyribonucleic Acid and Protein Structures," in *Nature*, vol. 173 (February 1954), p. 318.

code."[12] In a letter to Watson and Crick, Gamow writes: "If your point of view is correct each organism will be characterized by a long number written in quadrucal (?) system with figures 1, 2, 3, 4 standing for different bases [...]. This would open a very exciting possibility of theoretical research based on combinatorix and the theory of numbers! [...] I have the feeling this can be done. What do you think?"[13]

Here, Gamow does not present the problem of the transfer of genetic information as one that could be solved purely by means of experimental molecular biology. He obviously thought that he was confronted with a fundamentally cryptological problem, and that this problem should be tackled with cryptological and information theoretical methodology alone.

1953, the year Watson and Crick discovered the double helix, was also an important year in terms of politics. Stalin died in March; on June 17th the people of the German Democratic Republic stood up against their government; in July the Korean War found its end; and the Soviet Union tested its first hydrogen bomb. In the United States, national security was the highest priority on the political agenda. Encryption technologies and computer-assisted information theory, were booming, especially in the military domain. At the time, collaborating with the military was all the rage. George Gamow is an ideal example of this collaboration. In addition to his professorship at George Washington University, he also worked as a consultant for the United States Navy Bureau of Ordnance, the Air Force Scientific Advisory Board, and the Los Alamos Scientific Laboratory.

Due to the huge interest that scientists such as Gamow had for biological questions and in particular for a biological code, the topoi of information theory, linguistics, and cryptology began to spread in molecular biology and thus started to contribute to a "reconfiguration" (Kay) of biology. The storage and transfer of genetic information became a central object of biological research.[14]

12 RNA is also a nucleic acid and structurally very similar to DNA. During the protein synthesis, a complimentary RNA molecule is synthesized from a section of DNA, which then serves as a model for the synthesis of the amino acid chain.

13 Quoted from Kay, footnote 2, p. 131.

14 Gamow himself also considered the term "information" valid for the question of how biological specificity was maintained. "We use the term 'information' in the sense of a molecular specificity, that which distinguishes one protein from another." George Gamow, Alexander Rich, and Martynas

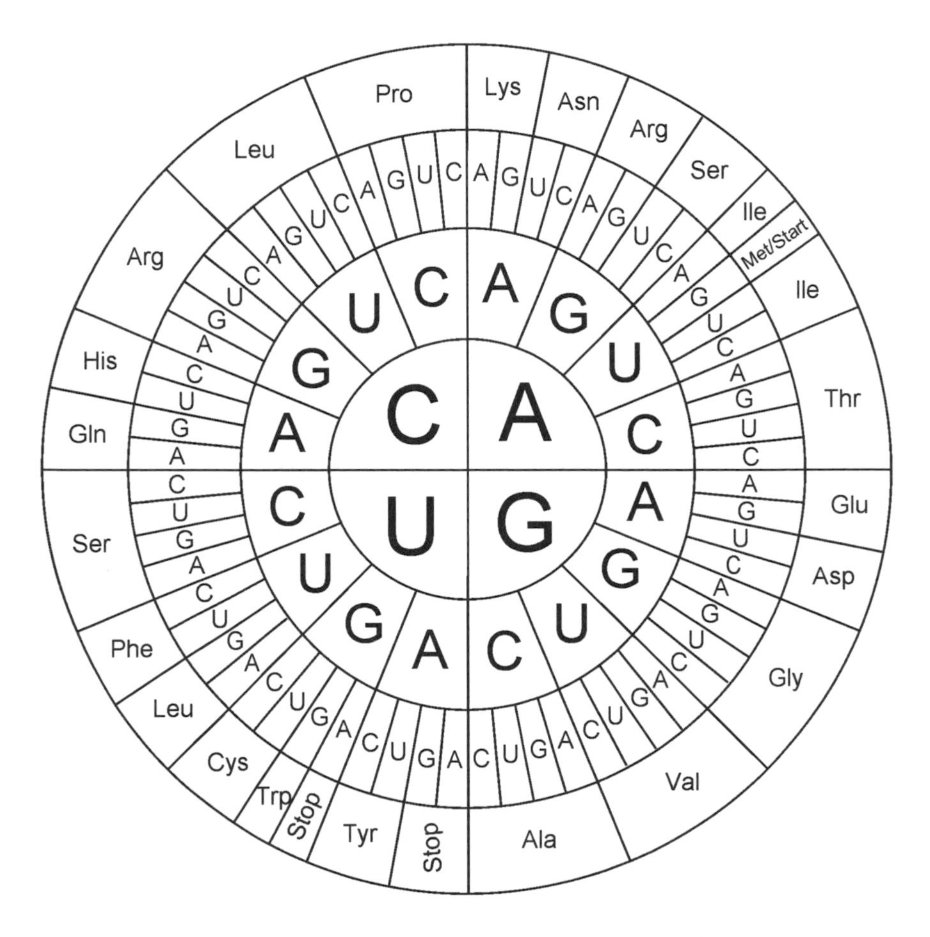

Fig. 3: The genetic code. Reading example: the base sequence UUU on the RNA (read from inside) codes for the amino acid phenylalanine (Phe). Nirenberg und Matthaei discovered this in their Poly(U) experiment. The three codons UGA, UAG, and UAA do not code for an amino acid; they signal the interruption of the protein synthesis. Each coded section on the DNA is completed by one of these three codons.

The so-called "coding problem" became concrete with the question of how a long sequence out of four bases determines a protein sequence consisting of twenty amino acids. Gamow's first approach to this problem was published in 1954 in *Nature*. His "diamond code" was an overlapping triplet code. Overlapping, because the last base of a triplet was the first base of the following triplet [Fig. 2]. The term diamond code can be explained by the fact that Gamow imagined the relationship between DNA and amino acid sequences as a lock-and-key relationship. The furrows in the DNA helix encircled by four nucleic bases resemble the form of a tetrahedron. According to Gamow, each furrow's border would determine, for geometrical reasons, which amino acid fits into the gap, thereby establishing the complementarity of base triplets and amino acids. Despite the fact that Gamow's suggestion proved empirically unsustainable, his efforts to find a solution for the coding problem formed the conceptual background against which deciphering the genetic code became a central issue of biology throughout the 1950s.[15]

The second decisive phase of research into the genetic code began when scientists attempted to decipher the code not purely theoretically, but also by means of experimental biochemistry. In 1961, Marshall Nirenberg and Heinrich Matthaei reached a decisive breakthrough. In a cell-free in-vitro system, using synthetic ploy(U)RNA (a long RNA chain that contains only uracil), they managed to synthesize a chain of amino acids which consisted of only one kind of amino acid: phenylalanine.[16] Now, the first base triplet (UUU) was clearly attributed to the corresponding amino acid (phenylalanine). Further experimental successes ultimately led to the full mapping of all possible triplets and, hence, completed the genetic code [Fig. 3].

So, again, is the term genetic code purely a metaphor, or is it not? Should we not think of the relationship between DNA and protein as strictly causal, one that could be described just as well with less intentional terms like "code," "information," or "translation"?

Yčas, "The Problem of Information Transfer from Nucleic Acids to Proteins," in *Advances in Biological and Medical Physics* 4 (1956), pp. 23–68.

15 See Kay, footnote 2, chap. 4 for the relevance of the "formalistic phase" in the history of the genetic code.

16 See Marshall Nirenberg's Nobel Prize speech, *The Genetic Code. Nobel Lecture,* 1968, online: www.nobelprize.org.

Hans Blumenberg, in his *Paradigmen zu einer Metaphorologie* (Paradigms for a Metaphorology), outlines two views that should be considered with respect to metaphors: The first proposes that metaphors are "*leftover elements* [...], rudiments on the path from *mythos to logos*[.]"[17] From this perspective, metaphors are used wherever our vocabulary is not yet mature enough to formulate all our knowledge in a positive and strictly rational manner. Thus, metaphors are mere linguistic tools that are employed as long as we are unable to use our words in a nonfigurative, or literal sense. In this view, metaphors "indicate the Cartesian provisionality of the historical situation [...]," which can be "measured against the regulative ideality of the pure logos."[18] Any critical examination of metaphors from this first perspective would fulfill an unveiling function. Consequently, "metaphorology would here be a critical reflection charged with unmasking and counteracting the inauthenticity of figurative speech," and would expose it as such.

However, the second perspective sees metaphors as "the *foundational elements* of language."[19] It assumes that metaphors, in order to be meaningful, need not necessarily have to be re-translateable into authentic or unambiguous language. Metaphoric language should not be measured against the ideal of pure logicality. In this sense, metaphors (Blumenberg calls them "absolute metaphors") possess a "conceptually irredeemable expressive function." The use of absolute metaphors is therefore not affected by the flaws of inauthentic speech, but rather these metaphors generate an independent mode of authenticity. Every conceptual analysis of an absolute metaphor would aim at the disclosure of the independent expressive function of the metaphor in question. The decisive ramifications of the second perspective is that the "equivalence of figurative and 'inauthentic' speech proves questionable," which ultimately boils down to the insight that the difference between figurative, metaphorical speech and nonfigurative, literal speech can no longer be sustained as such.

In his metaphorology, Blumenberg is mainly interested in *philosophical* language. However, similar questions can be formulated with respect to *scien-*

17 See Hans Blumenberg, *Paradigms for a Metaphorology*, trans. with an afterword by Robert Savage, Ithaca (forthcoming in 2010).
18 Ibid.
19 Ibid.

tific language: Does using metaphors in science serve a purely heuristic function at the beginning of a new scientific paradigm, and do metaphors, in the course of time vanish from a theory's vocabulary? Can all the metaphors of a mature theory be replaced by well-defined technical terminology? Is a theory at its peak if it no longer requires the use of metaphors? Or do metaphors play a fundamental and irreplaceable role in science? Is it possible that the elimination of metaphors always means a certain conceptual loss for the corresponding theory – so that, in other words, the theory, after translating all of its metaphors, would no longer be the same theory? If the term "genetic code" is a metaphor, can it be replaced by a literal term? Or does the expression "genetic code" possess a literal, irreducible meaning that need not be mated with other contexts in which the term "code" is used?

Questions such as these are very difficult to answer, particularly because, as already mentioned, the term "code" possesses so many nonscientific connotations, yet, nonetheless, perfectly describes the relationship between DNA and protein sequences. But if one takes Hans Blumenberg's alternative not only as an opportunity to pose interesting *theoretical* questions, but as a *real* alternative that demands a decision – and, moreover, if one actually decides to assume the second perspective *de facto,* which goes along with ignoring the difference between authentic and inauthentic speech regarding the code metaphor in biology – then the knowledge-catalytic function of the code metaphor as an autonomous and non-reducible signifier comes to the fore. Under this precondition, the above questions loose much of their edge. If one does not question how, today, after the cracking of the code, the code metaphor and the talk of genetic information can best be transformed to a non-metaphoric language, but, instead, considers the horizon of independent meanings that these "absolute" metaphors have generated throughout their long history, then one inevitably discovers the very inspiring and innovative effect they have had in the concerned fields of science. Would George Gamow have been so persistent in attempting to solve the "coding problem" of biology if he, as a physicist, had not previously been so involved with problems concerning information theory and military cryptology? And would Marshall Warren Nirenberg and Heinrich J. Matthaei have made the decisive experimental efforts to discover the complete genetic code and the mechanisms of protein synthesis if Gamow and others had not done the necessary theoretical groundwork? What would have happened had information metaphor never found its way into molecular biology? The counterfactual character of this kind of historical questions might be disillusioning, because they already imply the impossibility of being answered. We simply cannot know what would have happened if... Nevertheless, it can be said that although the early theoretical attempts and the extensive use of the information-theoretical vocabulary itself did not lead directly to deciphering the genetic code, they nonetheless made a vital contribution to the decisive experiments in the early 1960s, which ultimately paved the way for the well confirmed and wide knowledge of the present. Perhaps the extensive use of linguistic and informational metaphors was not necessary for that, but it was helpful in any case.

Gabriele Gramelsberger

STORY TELLING WITH CODE

Operating a coffee machine or a dryer is a matter of pushing the right button and the right time. We would never even consider talking to or giving instructions to them. Pushing the button activates the machine's mechanical or electric system.

Computers are an entirely different story. Even if we are not aware of it, we are constantly communicating with these machines, whether we are surfing the net, downloading an image, or writing a text. We are giving instructions to the computer hoping that the machine correctly understands what we want which is not always the case. Failed communication and obstinate interpretations are day-to-day occurrences – and then we lose control, screaming and cursing at these dreary machines. But how did we so willingly adapt to talking to machines, either silently via the keyboard, or even verbally? How far does this communication actually extend between humans and machines, senses and signals, desires and codes? What new possibilities can be extracted from this particular type of communication? First clarifying and explaining the make up of the computer could aid in answering these questions. Very few of us have ever unscrewed the computer body to peek inside. Yet, even if we did, we would only register a couple of helpful clues. One reason for this is the miniaturization of the most vital components, another is the fact that the computer does not produce anything really tangible, like coffee or dry washing. It deals in symbols that it generates, stores, and deletes. Or even more precisely, it deals in an overwhelming number of zeros and ones, or states of electricity flow that we trigger every day. Yet, we barely notice any of these basal processes today.

A Short History of Programming

Plug-n-Play

It was a very different case when computers burst onto the scene in the 1940s. Back then, the user had to actually enter inside the computer to turn it on. *ENIAC (Electronic Numerical Integrator and Computer)* for example, one of the first electronic computers, was a massive creature containing almost 18,000 vacuum pipes. Despite its size, its memory was only capable of storing a few hundred symbols. And it could only operate by means of hundreds of plugs.

"Plug-n-play" was very hard work back then and it took days to set up the *ENIAC* before it could perform the necessary calculations. "Setting up the ENIAC meant plugging and unplugging a maze of cables and setting arrays of switches. In effect, the machine had to be rebuilt for each new problem it was to solve."[1] Machine communication meant translating instructions directly into a configuration of interconnections: each new task led to a new configuration in the machine. A mathematical task was broken down into sequences of instructions that corresponded to the plugs.[2] In order to plug in the mass amount of connections properly, operators made notes on paper in the form of simple commands, such as "S*(x)* A*c*: Clear accumulator and add number located at position x in the Sceletrons into it."[3] Even if the term "programming" was not yet in use, this conceptual, manual act of writing with a pencil on paper marks the beginning of the development of the code.

In the 1947 report entitled *Planning and Coding Problems for an Electronic Computing Instrument,* John von Neumann and Herman Goldstine, who contributed to developing the *ENIAC,* established a definition for the term *coding:* The organizing of a task into a series of steps and the translation of these steps into a sequence of commands for a machine. This translation process entailed ensuring that the commands did in fact correspond to the task, and that each command was the inevitable consequence of the one that preceded it. A gap in the command sequence would crash the computer. They recommended a graphic method that would simplify the concept of command sequence: "Coding begins with the drawing of the flow diagrams. This is the dynamic or macroscopic stage of coding. [...] It has been our invariable experience, that once the problem has been understood and prepared [...], the drawing of the flow diagram presents little difficulty."[4] These flow diagrams specified which calculations occurred in which sequence, in which parts of the memory the results would be stored, and which routines would be repeated. The result was an intri-

1 Paul E. Ceruzzi, *A History of Modern Computing,* Cambridge/Mass., 1998, p. 21.

2 The first computers were pure calculators. The age of information processing began when computers and their memory capabilities became more powerful.

3 Herman H. Goldstine, John von Neumann, "Planning and Coding Problems for an Electronic Computing Instrument," Part II, vol. 1, 1948, in John von Neumann: *Collected Works,* vol. 5, Oxford etc., 1963, pp. 80–151, here: p. 85.

4 Ibid., p. 100.

cate choreography of branching command paths and loops. The code, in effect, was a symbolic instruction fed into the machine, which then was carried out in real operations. Since the first computer commands followed the principle of basic computer architecture directly, which broke down complex mathematical functions into simple basic functions, the codes were purely for the machine and impenetrable for the user. For example, the machine code 00 W0 03 W0 01 Z1 corresponded with the mathematical term i = i-1.[5] This is why the first problems that could be solved by the computer were pure calculation problems. Indeed, *ENIAC* could do this very well as long as it was wired to solve a particular mathematic problem. It took only two seconds to solve a problem for which a human "computer" would need seven hours. In other words, business with this massive creature and the tedious communication was well worth it, even in the 1940s. Moreover, the military was especially interested in this mechanical computing machine, first for calculating ballistics for bombs, later for missiles, and then for other fields.

Coding Instead of Instructing

Coding, as described by Goldstine and von Neumann in 1947, remained manual work well into the 1950s, performed with pencil on paper in the form of machine codes. Even the smallest command had to be rewritten for every single new task. Yet the majority of coding consisted of standard routines that were repeated in the same progressions and were highly time-consuming for the computer to solve and the programmers to prepare and enter. Hence, the decisive step to programming evolved precisely from the automation and mechanization of the coding itself. Rather than organizing each mathematical operation into steps manually and then formulating this into a machine language, a program was developed to translate the desired operations automatically into a machine code. The development of compilers was the first step in this direction. These were programs that translated commands into machine codes.[6] Yet it would still be a while before Compiler and other programming

5 See Donald E. Knuth and Luis Trabb Pardo, "The Early Development of Programming Languages," in *A History of Computing in the Twentieth Century*, ed. by N. Metropolis, J. Howlett, and Gian-Carlo Rota, New York, etc., 1980, pp. 197–273, here: p. 214.

6 Halcomb Laning and Neal Zierler developed the first algebraic compiler for WHIRLWIND in 1954 at the Massachusetts Institute for Technology.

tools could be applied: "At that time [1954], most programmers wrote symbolic machine instructions exclusively [...] they firmly believed that any mechanical coding method would fail to apply the versatile ingenuity which each programmer felt he possessed and constantly needed in his work."[7]

The first real, implemented programming language was *FORTRAN (Formula Translation).* It was introduced in 1954 by John Backus and is still used today in the natural sciences. According to Backus, the development of *FORTRAN* is based on the question regarding "what could be done now to ease the programmer's job? Once asked, the answer to this question had to be: Let him use mathematical notations. But behind that answer [...] there was the really new and hard question: Can a machine translate a sufficiently rich mathematical language into a sufficiently economical machine program to make the whole affair feasible?"[8] The last question was anything but trivial, for it was necessary to ensure that the computer actually did execute the programmed calculation. If the programmers themselves translated their calculations into machine commands, they could also personally verify them. Yet, if the translation were delegated to a programming language or a compiler, the programmers would then have to rely on a programming tool. *FORTRAN* provided a simple and reliable way to render the previously hand-coded machine commands of mathematical calculations in standard mathematical notation like addition (SUM) or the calculation of functions (COS, SIN, and so on). *FORTRAN* prevailed in the natural sciences and engineering, despite the fact that other programming languages also were developed, such as MATH-MATIC by Grace Hopper for UNIVAC, which was provided with the IBM 704 computers from 1957 onward.

Programming

The definitive advancement of the 1950s was not only the automatization of coding by Compilers and the first programming languages, but rather the introduction of mathematical modes of speaking with machines. Taking the

7 John Backus and W. P. Heising, "FORTRAN," in *IEEE Transactions on Electron Devises* 13 (1964): pp. 382–385, here: p. 382.

8 John Backus, "Programming in America in the 1950s — Some Personal Impressions," in *A History of Computing in the Twentieth Century,* ed. by N. Metropolis, J. Howlett, and Gian-Carlo Rota, New York, 1980, pp. 125–135, here, p. 131.

step of translating from programmer code to machine code – in the form of a *higher programming language* – meant treading the path from hardware to software. The purpose of these first programming languages was to formulate solutions to mathematical problems. But it soon became obvious that computers, particularly as they grew more and more powerful, were capable of much more than calculating[9] because computers could be used in two different ways: they could calculate, but they could also perform logical operations; they completed procedures and processed data. From the 1970s on, the data processing of information, texts, became increasingly important. Under these circumstances, the "mathematic" language might in effect be simpler than a machine code. Yet programming, as we know it today, is based on everyday codes that can not only calculate, but also perform increasingly complex information processing tasks. This shifts the "focus from designing programs to organizing data."[10] Now prefabricated programs have made computers more user-friendly and, consequently, fit for mass production. The average computer user is no longer active on the level of codes – neither machine codes nor programming codes – he or she works on the surface of the program and operates precoded applications. This marks another translation phase that leads from the machine code, to the program code, to the application, and back again – because every application has to be translated back into the program, and then ultimately the machine code. This final translation phase to the pure application, meant the disappearance of not only the actual machine, but also its logical and mathematical operating modes, behind the colorful interface of the application program and its penetration into offices and homes. With the

9 In 1960, the PDP-1 was built. It was the first computer that cost less than one million dollars to build. In 1961, the first integrated circuit was available on the market and paved the way for miniaturization. The computer mouse was developed in 1968 in Xerox Parc. In 1969, the first mainframe computers were networked (ARPANET) and, thus, the first data communication system. In 1971, Intel presented the first microprocessor, and Texas Instruments built the first single-chip computer. In 1972, Nolan Bushnell invented the first computer game. In 1977, Xerox introduced the first PC, followed by Apple in 1978. This marked the onset of personal computers in the home, such as the C64 by Commodore in 1982, Lisa by Apple in 1983, or likewise in 1983, XT by IBM. Home computers then cost between 1500 and 2000 DM (approx. 630 to 840 dollars), and mainframes for science and industry between 30 and 50 million DM (approx. 12.5 to 21 million dollars). In 1993 ARPANET was renamed Internet, and was being used more and more by the business sector. The World Wide Web was introduced in 1994. See Hans H. Hiebel, *Kleine Medienchronik,* Munich, 1997.

10 Georg Trogemann and Jochen Viehoff, *CodeArt,* Vienna, New York, 2005, p. 161.

computer's conquest of so many areas of personal and professional life, the improvement of computer graphics technology and the networking of computers, computer logic has triumphed worldwide and standardized the organization of work processes, the conditions of communication, and the way we think. This standardization is now called "programming." And it almost seems as though the only things still considered relevant nowadays are those that can be programmed – and thus forced into a system of functions and data. And curiously enough, the more influential computer logic becomes, the more it disappears from our direct perception – both because of miniaturization and the given features of the applications. Glancing at the history of computer and software development clearly shows that computers are first and foremost machines, then mathematical machines, and lastly, the text and image machines as we know and use them today. Yet this overlapping of different layers of mechanical dimensions is important for our understanding of what constitutes a code, that is, what can be programmed and thus created. Frolicking on the surface of these applications will never help us understand the vast potential of this machine.

Digital Narration

One potential that has emerged over the last few years is the ability to "tell stories" using code. It is a very specific and innovative manner of narration, and considering the omnipresence of the computer, now a very powerful narrative form of modern society. What is meant here is not so much the virtual worlds of computer games or other immersive environments – which are also new forms of narration – or the floods of hypertexts or the Internet as a narrative network. This is about a new form of narrating our own lives, and it is changing our everyday experience as well as our relationship to the world: it is the logic of the computer that is increasingly penetrating and modifying reality in new ways and, thus, creating narratives. The ability to "tell stories" using code is exported from the computer into the environment and, in this way, creates unexpected, new possibilities and horizons. Examples for these new ways of using computers include the molecular design of new materials, new design idioms[11] like

11 This mode of application has always been an integral part of the computer, due to its mathematical nature, but it only became actually possible since the 1990s when the computer and its visualization technologies became more powerful.

those in architecture, for instance, or, in the future, maybe even new forms of life. This new way of using computers will become feasible once not only the act of designing is computer based, but also all modes of production necessary to manipulate material entities, be they cells, materials, or components. At the very latest, when the *digital chain* is complete, computer logic will reach out to the material world and redesign it within the framework of this logic. In architecture, the use of this *digital chain* can be seen in Frank O. Gehry's work. However, what Gehry does primarily is transfer conventional design practice into the digital, using a program called *CATIA*, in order to realize complex architectural forms structurally that are designed first in a conventional manner using models and paper. Yet digital logic promises much more, as the different approaches by Frank O. Gehry and Peter Eisenman illustrate. "While Gehry used the computer as a pragmatic tool, Eisenman saw it as a conceptual starting point for new projects. Wanting to liberate himself from the Cartesian absolute of a priori formal beauty, Eisenman used the computer to explore more dynamic, less predictable patterns of organization. He wants to release architecture from the restrictions of its fixation on objects in order to arrive at a textual architecture."[12] Overcoming the Cartesian absolute motivates a new narration of the world and allows a new manner of communication with the material environment. Different types of this story telling with code can be distinguished. First there is an indirect version that changes the form of material but not its actual structure – there are very good examples of this in architecture and technology. And there is a direct version that changes the "natural" code, the DNA – as can be seen in synthetic biology and nanotechnology. It will be even more interesting when both versions come together, for instance, when new materials interact with new architectural design idioms.

Parametric Design

Parametric design will enable us to observe these new forms of narration more carefully. The computer will again be used primarily as a mathematical machine, consistent with its initial nature, and not as a drawing board. Returning to the computer as a mathematical tool opens up a new degree of liberty

12 Translated from Anette LeCuyer, "Entwerfen am Computer: Frank Gehry und Peter Eisenman," in *arch+* 128 (1995), pp. 26–29, here: p. 28.

when generating new design idioms, because the digital drawing board imitates conventional design on paper using compasses, rulers, and other tools and their Cartesian systems of coordination. There are of course added functional tools, but the basic principles of designing on paper, such as Euclidian or projective geometry, are taken on and adapted accordingly: objects are constructed from lines and surfaces and thus fill an empty space that stretches through a system of coordinates. Depending on the calculated angle of perspective, the impression of a three-dimensional presentation is created on a flat screen from the two dimensional elements. Rapid prototyping allows such presentations to be easily printed as a three-dimensional model. Yet the orientation on traditional design is unnecessarily restrictive for the design idiom. The transformation to the digital does not really add anything new; it is subjected to the logic of the paper surface more than to the logic of the computer and its n-dimensional, relational data space. Michael Silver describes this ambivalent state between paper and computer as follows: "Aside from its visual complexity, the resulting work shows little evidence of the computer's role in the creation of underlying principles. [...] Because the tools themselves offer little surprise, information [...] is defined as a disembodied content that travels unchanged between different media (from physical models to scanned data sets, to built forms, etc.). [...] Materials are understood as passive receptors of a code that reflects as closely as possible a sculptural idea formulated in advance."[13]

In computer logic designing is something entirely different. It means generating new forms on the basis of algebraic and arithmetic operations. In contrast to the geometry of conventional architectural design, which is based essentially on lines and surfaces, algebraic forms of every kind are generated from one point and its trajectory (the path of the point's development in the given period). In other words, the world is no longer narrated from the perspective of the surface or the objects, but rather generated outward from a specific point. And this new method of narration holds the potential for even further narrations, for when buildings and objects become masses of accumulated points and bundles of trajectories, the relation between these points and the trajectories' path of development can be redefined again and again. This is

13 Michael Silver, "Matter/in-formation," in *Autogenic Structures,* ed. by Evan Douglis, New York, 2008, pp. 152–191, here: p. 154.

exactly where the computer code comes in, by allowing the new design principles that are not based on geometry to affect the points and trajectories. The object is thus understood as a system of elements that are affected by forces. New forms can be generated according to the selected parameters and specifications, and how the forces or rules of production work. In the process certain arrangements create their own design idiom: examples include fractal forms, L-systems, swarm algorithms, and mechanical force simulators.

Designing in this manner might slightly delegate some authorship to a machine, yet this is compensated by the gained freedom of formal language this method can offer. This design method also exploits the idiosyncrasy of the computer. Algebra and arithmetic take the place of geometry. Because even when objects or curves are generated from masses of points, a mathematical point is still very different from one that is drawn. Essentially, a mathematical point is nothing more than a dimensionless, numerical value on a specific point in a matrix. Manipulating these numerical values changes curves, object surfaces, and, hence, forms. This shifts the time-based character of this design approach to the fore. Forms are not constructed by means of lines, circles, or squares, or other preexisting templates, but rather evolve during the work process. A temporary form is created whenever the program is paused. The form is then completed according to the way in which information in the form of parameters is fed to and stored in the temporary form. Any information, which can be presented as a numerical value, can influence the temporary form as a parameter. This might be information about the planned building, such as traffic volume, gravity, or the shapes of other buildings. Or, to refer to an example by Peter Eisenman from the 1990s, the turbulence of a river flowing around the house: "This design began with cubes shaped by *solitons;* a dynamic system that borders on chaos. Single waves are physical phenomena – which seem coincidental, but in fact are caused by calculable physical factors – that are caused by sudden changes in deep water or in underground seismographic occurrences in water. Solitons are created by doubling single waves. They are energy impulses that pass through solid bodies, fluids, or gasses and create nonlinear interactions."[14] These interactions appear as deformations on the

14 LeCuyer, footnote 12, p. 28. Anette LeCuyer is referring to Eisenman's project "Haus Immendorf" in Dusseldorf.

cube and thus generate a new, unpredictable form, and they can only be discovered via the computer. The form thus generated tells a story about the contextual environment. In this way, the story of the environment is stored in the form. This type of narration illustrates the new and far-reaching future influence the computer will have on day-to-day life as *story telling with code.* If buildings designed in this manner are realized, a new way of reading and taking these buildings in will be needed. Their code cannot be as easily deciphered as the code that is used for conventional formal standards. Yet in the future, new materials and new communication technologies will make it easier to read the contextuality and, hence, narration of these new objects. However, new materials will also add to the evolution of form as a dynamic entity in the constructed reality. Even more possibilities can be imagined: in the future, the built object will no longer be an instantaneous state of a temporary shape fixed in time, but the building of the future may even be capable of changing its form in real time.

The Natural Sciences and Computers

Using computers to generate new forms and new design idioms with parametric design has long been working practice in natural science computer laboratories everywhere. And, in fact, for some years this is where the parametric design of nature has been closely studied using computer simulations of climate, cell, or molecular simulation. This method has allowed the natural sciences to fall back on a powerful design principle that was discovered in the seventeenth century: the mechanics and dynamics of physical processes. For instance, the simulated model of the atmosphere in weather or climate models is a programmed, mechanical atmosphere consisting of thousands of fluids (non-expandable particles). The model simulates the forces that affect such fluids according to dynamic and physical principles. In this simulation the measured data input into the simulated system has an influence on the results. Because the natural sciences are more interested in processes than in forms, the result of such a simulation is a prognosis of how processes might conceivably develop, for example, in order to predict the weather. However, they could also represent forces that can distort the atmosphere, like weather reports create visualizations of turbulence, air mass formations, or weather conditions.

It is interesting to note that the scientific contribution of the seventeenth century went beyond Isaac Newton's deciphering of physical design principles.

The true breakthrough of this new science of physics was the invention of an innovative mathematical method called *differential calculus,* which allowed processes in space and time to be visualized and made infinitesimal processes manageable. Differential calculus allowed modern science to overcome geometry and, thus, the static presentation of natural forms that ancient mathematics produced with lines drawn by rulers and compasses – a method that ultimately constructed geometric objects. An example of this conception of nature can be seen in medieval images of the cosmos with planetary orbits that corresponded to platonic bodies.

With differential calculus, nature is conceived from one mathematical point, which is affected by different forces. These influences generate the trajectories of a system that develops exclusively as paths or curves from one point. The point stores the coding of its development, so to speak, and develops it further in the course of the calculation or simulation. "The graphic geometric line is dissolved by the virtue of this process into a sequence of numeric values that are related by a specific arithmetic rule."[15] The natural sciences made this step from *object,* or "substance," as termed by Ernst Cassirer, to *function* over the course of the seventeenth century. Since replacing geometry with algebra and arithmetic was a computationally intensive substitution – because even a single line or curve consists of an infinite number of points – automatic calculating machines became necessary in order to effectively calculate systems which consisted of millions of points. This is, in effect, the origin of the computer, as a purely mathematic machine, and the motivational basis to build automatic calculating machines in the 1940s. The enormous increase in the power and graphics capacity of the computer since the 1970s, and especially since the 1990s, now conveys this transformation of classic formal standards of geometry in mathematic points and trajectories beyond the natural sciences, namely to architecture – making it possible to tell new stories about nature, environment, technology, and architecture.

15 Ernst Cassirer, *Substance and Function, and Einstein's Theory of Relativity* (1910), Chicago, London, 1923.

Georg Trogemann

CODE AND MACHINE

In computer science, codes are related to the triangulum *communication – message – information.* The one common basis for these terms is the semiotic analysis of communication processes, which assumes that all communication can be considered a transmission of messages. In this context, any form of presenting a message is a code and every system of symbols – that is supposed to represent and transmit the information between sender and receiver via a predetermined agreement – is called a "code." In a strictly mathematical context, a code is a directive that allows symbols of a coded set of characters to be classified in a clear and precise manner. The objective of a computer science coding theory is to create the *fastest, most accurate,* and *most efficient* methods to store and transmit messages of different origin using the appropriate symbol systems. The term code is applied here in two ways, first for the mathematical mapping, and second for the chain of characters created by the coding.

This essay will not attempt to outline the inner structure of a symbol, in other words, how symbols relate to each other, or the mapping between coded sets of characters, nor will we observe specific coding processes or formal languages and their advantages and disadvantages. We will instead focus on how codes develop their force within the overall configuration of today's computer architecture. Before the 1970s, the only thing considered economically lucrative in the field of computer practice was the expensive hardware – programs were little more than free supplements. But today almost the opposite is true. The world of computers is now defined by *floating codes* that move freely through networks; the inexpensive hardware is an environment that is purely optional. Cloud computing is the next phase of computer networking. In this paradigm, users need not know where the program codes are calculated or where data is stored. The World Wide Web not only shapes the global economy; it shapes our perception and intellect more and more – even reality as a whole seems computer generated. Codes in terms of source code or program code, meaning algorithms written by the same rules of actual program languages, play the decisive role here.

Code and Perception

"Ultimately, everything will succumb to the power of algorithms."[1] *Frieder Nake*

Programs are becoming inescapable assistants that mainly help to produce new knowledge and methods needed, for instance, to develop new materials, solve complex mathematical problems, or simulate climates. Yet, not only science or engineering depends on different software tools, but also classic creative disciplines such as design and architecture. How did the code grow to become so omnipresent and what hidden influence do they have on the results of the work process?

Symbols became independent as an inevitable consequence of the complete process of axiomatization and formalization in mathematics and its logical application in the natural sciences. Before David Hilbert, symbols had a reference to the world, albeit a loose one. While Euclidian geometry was still attempting to define a point and a straight line, mathematician David Hilbert from Göttingen was following a very formal approach to axiomatics. Hilbert was interested only in the links; the objects themselves remained undefined and were mechanically provided with geometry-related names. Hilbert himself claimed that it should always be possible to say, "table," "chair," and "beer mug" instead of "point," "straight," or "plane." His strictly formal approach was an attempt to base mathematics on a consistent system of axioms, and to rid the world once and for all of any doubt about the certainty of mathematical deduction. In Hilbert's Program symbols were still connected to truths in the world. Yet the postmodernists completely rejected any claim to truth in semiotic representations. Codes now formed their own truths; they no longer represented the world, but themselves. They became placeholders for unknown content, and working with them was limited to a schematic handling of symbols. Relationships between symbols and the observed phenomenon were subjected purely to expedience and no longer required universality. Pragmatism appropriated truth. Yet this aspect of the restriction of claims to truth is only one side of the coin, it underestimates the actual reality generated by the symbols themselves.

1 Quoted from the lecture "WolkenBilder, wolkig," (Cloud pictures, cloudy) given at *HyperKult 18* in Lüneburg on July 4, 2009.

Formal systems are grounded in mathematics, yet they nevertheless function at a level on which members of a society can relate to each other, despite their many differences. Every thinking subject has access to this general rationality. If enough people think in a rational way, it will inevitably become public and social thinking. The only requirement needed for this form of public thinking is the ability to abstract, which is the individual starting point. In this respect, any rational knowledge available in coded form will become public and objective knowledge, as long as it can be understood by everyone who is able to read the formal codes. Hence, rational processes that are delegated to machines are a form of an objective theory of action. Holling and Kempin[2] call them "implemented theories," whereby they define "implementation" as the general execution of a formal process by a machine. This makes implemented theories a subset of those theories that are characterized by being *operable.* Both authors refer to the fact that there is a long tradition behind underestimating the formal – but not only in the arts and humanities, which viewed formalism as a limited tool used in the natural sciences, but in mathematics as well, which also attaches no social importance to its codes. However, both sides overlook the real significance of the formal as a social integration apparatus, and as an implemented theory. Although formal codes spread like wildfire with the increase of computers, they are still invisible and unobserved.

We would like to examine how it is possible for thought processes to be conveyed to machines in the first place: the thought process first has to be translated into a mechanical process of action. This gives the formalization the decisive role of mediator. Formalisms serve the precise symbolic description of methods, whereby methods in terms of formalism are nothing more than rules for our actions that allow us to select a specific action from many different alternatives. Previously analyses are functionalized by formal structures and, thus, translated into a learnable inventory of knowledge and to a transmittable process. "Formalization is nothing more than the most manageable way of functionalizing that which has already been established; but it could also be a process of mechanization, because whatever can be formalized – meaning, what its application gains notwithstanding the insightfulness of the execution

2 Eggert Holling, Peter Kempin, *Identität, Geist und Maschine – Auf dem Weg zur technologischen Gesellschaft,* Hamburg, 1989, p. 82.

– is already basically mechanized, even if the actual mechanisms needed for its storage and regulated association did not previously exist. All methodologies want to arrive at an unreflected repeatability, a growing archive of prerequisites that might always be in play, but do not always need to be updated.[3] We are now experiencing how our world is becoming ever more dominated by algorithms and – in the words of Frieder Nake – how everything, ultimately, is in fact succumbing to the power of algorithms. Yet in this context, the true significance of the code is its function as a social integration apparatus. That which has been coded, transmitted to thousand of machines, and has become a part of our day-to-day lives because it has been repeated again and again will stabilize and ultimately become a culturally unquestioned sediment. As an implemented and executable theory, the formal codes enter into an innovative and powerful relationship with the machine. Computers are not only the passive carriers of symbols, they are also active generators – symbols generate symbols. Yet it would be wrong to think that we would get the same phenomena back that we entered into the program during the design phase. The abstraction process needed to arrive at algorithms and operating symbols effectively runs backwards during the execution of the code, but not identically. If abstraction serves to withdraw, generalize, and purify the phenomena from insignificance and ambiguity, then, during execution, the program's corresponding interfaces recharge the results with the unintentional, the unfocused, and the ambiguous – for instance during the transition from image generating algorithms to the image itself. But that which has been charged is different to that which was discarded by means of abstraction, that is, on the path to algorithm.

Universality via Coding

"The importance of the universal machine is clear. We do not need to have an infinity of different machines doing different jobs. A single one will suffice. The engineering problem of producing various machines for various jobs is replaced by the office work of "programming" the universal machine to do these jobs."[4] *Alan Mathison Turing*

3 Translated from Hans Blumenberg, *Wirklichkeiten, in denen wir leben,* Ditzingen, 1981, p. 41.

4 Alan Mathison Turing, "Intelligent Machinery" (Prologue), in *Machine Intelligence 5,* ed. by Bernhard Meltzer and Donald Michie, Edinburgh, 1969, p. 7.

In the famous essay "On Computable Numbers, with an Application to the Entscheidungsproblem" Turing described the principle of the universal machine as follows: "It is possible to invent a single machine which can be used to compute any computable sequence. If this machine U is supplied with a tape on the beginning of which is written the D.N.[5] of some computing machine M then U will compute the same sequence as M."[6] Applied in a practical manner, this means that the list of instructions is coded for a specific Turing Machine *M* and writes this on the front of the tape. Coding means that, with a binary universal machine, we show the program as a sequence of zeros and ones, and not simply the data. This piece of tape is now the first part of the input for the universal Turing Machine *U*. It processes the remaining part of the tape by carrying out the instructions on the beginning of the tape and thus exactly imitates the specific machine *M*. In principle, today's programmable computers function along the same lines. They simulate the behavior of a specific machine by the program code being together with the data in the memory. Without software, the universal machine may be open for any conceivable behavior, but it is more or less incapable of action on its own. The universal machine begins behaving like a special machine, which is defined by the program, only after starting the program. Universal computers consist of two mechanical levels:
1. Hardware that is bound to conventional material.
2. The program codes that are only subjected to algorithmic laws.

The first level – the hardware – is bound to nature and obeys the laws of our physical world. It needs energy, is subjected to the aging process that will eventually lead to functional failure, and can be damaged by applied forces such as mechanical shocks, magnetism, and voltage surges. These material machines can execute logical elementary operations on the basis of physical principles. A second level sits on top of these electronic (mechanical, optical, and so on) machines that is not subject to physical laws, but instead is bound to human rationality and the limits of the formal. These code-based machines are beyond material weaknesses. They only know failures that can be traced back to a logical error on the part of the programmer. The code-based machine

5 D.N. = description number.

6 Alan Mathison Turing, "On Computable Numbers, with an Application to the Entscheidungsproblem," p. 241, quoted in: http://plms.oxfordjournals.org/cgi/reprint/s2-42/1/230 (accessed May 4, 2010).

brings the world of algorithms to fruition, it controls the performance of the bottom level, and is strictly bound to formal languages and the laws of human logic. New physical worlds, which are ruled by new and different natural laws, can be described on the machine's algorithmic level. We can delegate our reflections on the physical world to machines in the form of algorithms, and reencounter this logical construct in the simulation, but in completely new ways – no longer as a formally logical description, but as a total experience. The limits of this second machine go beyond our physical world; they lie in the limitations of codes and the human capacity to invent algorithmic worlds.

The Reflexive Properties of the Code

Both data and programs are coded in the programmable machine on the basis of identical symbols – consequently, these symbols are able to constantly enter into new relationships with one another. This is different in arithmetic, which makes a strict distinction between *operands* and *operators.* The computer can mechanically process data as well as programs. In architecture, for instance, architects design buildings, but in computer architecture, other computers actively help develop the next generation of computers. This is only possible because the code can switch functions. We can treat codes as data, but we can also actively manipulate them, meaning, they can become calculating units themselves. Any programs we download and start from websites are examples of *code as operand* and *code as operator.* The code is passive during the web transfer and treated as data by the network software. When the program is started on the computer, the code switches from operand to operator. As an operator, the code now manipulates data. The reflexive ability of the code is what enables the machine to become a practical entity. Without self-referential processing mechanisms, working on the computer would still be about zeros and ones. In order to explain the reflexive relationship between *code as operand* and *code as operator,* we would like to introduce two slightly complex examples: the compiler, and genetic programming.

Compilers are programs that contain symbols as entries (a program *a*) and use these to generate new symbols (program *a'*). The importance of the compiler's function is its ability to complete work in the first phase so that, in the second phase, the program can shift from the status of operand to operator. Compilers have to exist as a machine program in order to be run by a machine.

Creating them is a very time consuming and complex development process. Every compiler is specific to a single programming language *n* times a single machine language *m*. Therefore writing a compiler requires an amount of effort that increases exponentially with the numbers *n* and *m*. Clever use of the code's reflexive properties allows the compilers to translate themselves to a certain extent. The procedure is know as bootstrapping, and was developed very early in compiler history: from a compiler *a* designed for a specific implementation language and a specific Computer *A*, it easily creates a Compiler *b* for this implementation language on a Machine *B*.
1. In Compiler *a*, which already exists as code in the implementation language, the compiler creates the appropriate commands for Machine *B* everywhere the machine code for Machine *A* is created. This procedure produces the compiled code, named *a'*.
2. This code is translated by *A* and *a* into the Machine Code of *A* and results in a compiled code named *a"*.
3. *a"* is a program that can run on Computer *A*. Yet, this program receives *a'* as input and creates Machine Code *b*, which can run on Computer *B*. *B* is the desired compiler that runs on Computer *B* and creates programs that can also run on *b*.

The second example in this context is genetic programming. It belongs to the class of evolutionary algorithms that, as heuristic optimization algorithms, can offer good results even if there are no available closed solutions. They utilize the same properties of biological evolution based on populations of individuals that pass their genetic code on from generation to generation. The properties of each individual are encoded as genotypes. They represent the genetic construction of the individual and provide its blueprint. Generations are reproduced by a process of identical copying, the mutation of single chance positions of the code or the crossover of substructures between two individuals. Changes in the characteristics of an individual can only occur on the genotype (the chain of characters), but selection of the fittest according to the fitness function takes place on the phenotype. The phenotype is the physical manifestation of the genotype, that is, the specific characteristics of an individual in its environment. Special genotypes such as computer programs are worked on in genetic programming. The genotype in this context is the program code und the phenotype is the program's performance when it is running on a computer.

We can recognize even here the mechanism of the shift between *code as operator* and *code as operand.* The genotype functions as an operand for the basic genetic algorithm, and the phenotype of this code as the operator.

Automatic Self-Reproduction

This principle of genetic programming is also an example of the splitting of the universal computer into two machines, as described above. We acquire codes by means of evolutionary algorithms that are capable of manipulating themselves and further developing their performance. The lower level of the machine, the hardware that runs the genetic program, remains completely unaffected. In the following we will demonstrate that the spread of the code's self-manipulation strategies to the physical world is also used in the classic version by John von Neumann.

We first have to point out the sharp difference between self-replication and self-reproduction. Self-replication is a process by which an object creates a copy of itself. With regard to automatic replication by machines, this can be executed as a deterministic process in which it is particularly important that no flaws occur. Codes that exist as an explicit description of the machine are not needed in this case. In contrast, there is a possibility for diversity in "self-reproduction" as it implements a process of development that not only accepts, but also seeks variation and difference from generation to generation. Self-reproduction therefore is also a self-maintenance system that follows the Darwinian theory of evolution. Self-replication would not be sufficient to simulate life because it does not have any inherited mutations. To perform automatic self-reproduction, it would be useful if machines processed more than only the material in their environment to make copies of themselves, but also deal with specific information that exists in the form of codes. This does not mean any codes, but rather information with reflexive properties, that is, descriptions of their own construction. The first such process that allows more than simple self-replication, but also solves the evolutionary problem, can be traced to the mathematician John von Neumann.

This ability initially seems like a *circulus vitiosus,* because we would expect that the level of complexity of the systems that build other systems would decrease from *parents* to *offspring.* Automat *A* would need more than a complete description of Automat *B* in order to build *B*. It would also require different equipment that could interpret the description and carry out the construction work. Yet the initially plausible assumption that the complexity of self-building automats would decrease over generations is actually against the laws of nature's self-sustainability. Organisms reproduce and create new organisms that are at least as complicated as themselves. The level of complexity, as we know, can even increase over the course of a long evolutionary period.

But how can the general logical principles that allow automats to self-reproduce, and even increase in complexity, be described? Von Neumann's conclusion maintains that a minimal level of complexity is needed to allow automats to self-reproduce or to even create higher beings. Below this level, the automats are degenerative, meaning automats that build other automats are only capable of creating a less complex automat. John von Neumann observed five different models of self-reproduction. Arthur W. Burks named them the kinetic model, the cellular model, the excitation-threshold-fatigue model, the continuous model, and the probabilistic model.[7] The Turing Machine could not solve the problem of kinetic self-reproduction that we will examine more closely below, because it could only produce symbols in a piece of tape. However, with the kinetic model, von Neumann targets automats that build other automats, in other words, that do more than just manipulate symbols. They can also build hardware. The basic principle behind the kinetic system, von Neumann's focus of study since at least 1948, is not easily summarized. Von Neumann's self-reproducing automat is an aggregate consisting of three automats and their particular descriptions (blueprints).[8] First, a construction Automat *A* that is able to build any Automat *X* when given a description of Automat *F (X);* second, a copying Automat *B* that can make an identical copy from any description; and third, a control Automat *C* that monitors the interaction between Automats *A* and *B.* To begin, it activates Automat *A,* which immediately starts building Automat *X* according to the description *F (X).* Then, it activates Automat *B,* which produces a copy of *F(X).* This copy introduces C into the new Automat *X,* which was just built by A. Finally *C* separates the newly built Construction $X + F(X)$ from the construction automat.

7 See John von Neumann, *Theory of Self-Reproducing Automata,* ed. and completed by Arthur W. Burks, Urbana, 1966.

8 Georg Trogemann, Jochen Viehoff, *CodeArt – Eine elementare Einführung in die Programmierung als künstlerische Praktik,* Vienna, New York, 2005, pp. 443ff.

We can now call the entire Aggregate $A + B + C$ with D and get the desired self-reproduction Automat $D + F(D)$, whereby $F(D)$ is again a description of Automat D. What is significant about the von Neumann principle of self-reproduction is that it is impossible without coding. The machines have to be diverted by the coding of their own construction in order to be reproducible. Yet this means that Automat $D + F(D)$ does not only replicate itself – it actually possesses other important properties. We see for example that coincidental changes in $F(D)$ refer to characteristics that appear in biology in relation to mutations. Most random changes to $F(D)$ will render the automat inoperable. If there are enough changes, there will undoubtedly be several among them that will lead to new functional automats. These new automats possess different characteristics than their predecessors.

No changes in the description of the automat allow for a construction process that reproduces automats as well as by-products. Let E be the automat with the corresponding description $F(E)$; if we feed the above self-reproducing Automats $D = (A + B + C)$ with $F(A+ B + C + E)$, a new Automat $(A + B + C + D) + F(A + B + C + E)$ is created. The new automat does not only produce a copy of itself; it also generates an Automat E.

This play of automats no longer requires a user. Their duplication and further development becomes self-perpetual the moment the process is started. Ignoring for a moment the dangers inherent in surrendering all human control, this form of automatic autonomy is nevertheless undesirable for most work processes. Tools that expand the user's possibilities, and not the machine's, are far more interesting. The important issue here is how much will a programmer's decisions and the deterministic operating code be able to influence the desired result. How much creative space will software tools allow their users?

The Openness of Codes

A process can be formally described when it fulfills the conditions of writing, schematizing, and freedom of interpretation.[9] Writing means that the process can be expressed using symbols; schematizing means that the procedure can be described by a set schema and general processes (also algorithmic); and freedom of interpretation means that we are completely open to choose symbols

9 See Sybille Krämer, *Symbolische Maschinen*, Darmstadt, 1988, pp. 1–4.

and designations since we no longer refer to what the symbols represent while doing the operations. The process of formalizing has removed our need to understand on the level of symbols. A layperson can only understand what the symbols mean if he or she knows the key to the code. All of the three above-listed conditions of formalization are automatically fulfilled if the operation can be expressed in a program language readable by the machine. Formal structures, according to the present notions, leave little room to the imagination. Formalizing means that data is recorded as exactly as possible and that any misinterpretations or ambiguities can be rectified. The interesting question is where there might be space for participation and imagination when working on or with the computer. Does the formal, basic pattern of the computer and its programming only lead to stiff and uncreative results? Are architects who work with programs such as these at all free to decide and, hence, design, and if yes, to what extent? Have not all decisions once made by architects been specified in the tool, long before any individual production takes place? Is there still any space that allows for free designs that go beyond the settings made by the programmer?

When we speak of a program code being open, we are speaking very generally about features that allow new space for the users' action and interpretation, and that create a certain amount of flexibility and permeability for their intentions while working with the program. The program text, however, will always be the explicit and unambiguous given. On this level of description, freedom can only be achieved by introducing the self-changing strategies discussed above, like learning methods, self-references, or the general reflexive properties of the code. New things, or that, which the programmer assesses as unexpected, can only develop on the performative level of the code when the code writes itself. In fact, the openness of an application can be very easily achieved without any explicit changes made to the code in conventional applications. To achieve openness – according to the theory represented here – the qualities that should remain open should not be formalized. Here is an example taken from architecture.

Umberto Eco classifies architectural codes into syntactic and semantic categories.[10] Syntactic codes emulate the knowledge of constructions. They

10 Umberto Eco, *La struttura assente. La ricerca semiotica e il metodo strutturale,* Milan, 1968. The subsequent quote is translated from the German edition *Einführung in die Semiotik,* Munich, 1994, p. 329.

include beams, ceilings, arches, bearings, columns, and prefabricated concrete supporting structures. However, these syntactical codes do not yet refer to a function or a denoted space. This is achieved by semantic codes, which include primary functions such as roof, terrace, stairs, and window, but also domestic ideologies (communal room, day and evening zones, dining room, waiting room), *social typological genres* (hospital, villa, school, castle, train station), and *spatial typological genres* (round or cross shaped floor plans, labyrinths).

An architecture that works with codes such as these, according to Eco, cannot offer anything to their users that would not catch them off guard. "The common viewpoint regarding all of these codifications is that they give form to previous solutions, which means they are codifications of message types. [...] Hence, the codes [...] would be nothing more than iconic, stylistic, or rhetorical encyclopedic dictionaries. They do not offer any generative possibilities but rather a complete diagram, not open forms that can be discussed but hardened forms and general relationships of an unexpected kind. [...] It is not true that a few empty and purely differential forms of architectural import (columns and beams) make just any architectural statement: they specifically make the architectural statement to which Western civilization has accustomed us according to certain statistical and dynamic criteria and certain rules of Euclidian geometry. Even if they are more stable and more resistant to wear than other control systems, they still force us to operate within a specific architectural grammar. At least it is possible to find them codified under the term structural theory."[11] Architecture is not the only field that faces the challenge described by Eco, but anyone developing tools for open design processes. The implemented syntactic and semantic codes – called ontologies in the field of computer science – already decide which results are to be expected. If one wants a surprising result in relation to certain concepts, theories, and aesthetics, then they should precisely not be entered into the formalism of his or her system. If one does not want a building constructed of beams, ceilings, columns, and walls, then these should not be used as the basic elements of this design system either. What seems trivial here is nevertheless little reflected or even overcome in the available tools. Forfeiting familiar categories and concepts is certainly not very dif-

11 Ibid., p. 329ff.

ficult; the true challenge is shifting them to a different level of abstraction. Categories that should remain open need to be replaced by more abstract concepts, so they can be reconstructed as unique cases – they will remain unformalized, but are able to be created and reflected in the work process.

Claus Dreyer

ARCHITECTURAL CODES FROM A SEMIOTIC PERSPECTIVE

Despite the fact that the term "code" only surfaced recently in the field of architectural theory, it has a long tradition in the designing and realization of architecture in general. In the French and Anglo-American cultures, it refers to the system of laws and rules, the "codex," that established the standard norms, guidelines, and rules for every building within the scope of the relevant laws. This is what an English-speaking person means when using the term "building codes." Then there are "design codes" that refer to the diverse rules and conventions of architectural design, which are seldom strictly codified and follow traditional, cultural, conventional, and individual practices.[1] The following essay will address only these particular codes, because they played an important role in architecture and architectural theory during the second half of the twentieth century, the effect of which is still evident today.

In semiotics, the term "code" refers mainly to a specific, limited sign system that is used in context with comprehensive sign processes and systems, and that is defined and made operable by its particular characteristics – the rules that are applicable to allocation, replacement, and transformation play a vital role.[2] In particular, it is assumed from a sign system defined as "code" that the relationship between its repertory of signs and the accompanying meanings, if not yet institutionalized, is at least governed by approved conventions, so that the mechanisms of coding and decoding, plus the code transformation can be described and explained. This led to a great diversity in the definitions of codes that begin in general with equating it with "language" and then diverge infinitely in formal, functional, operational, habitual, social,

1 For more on this difference see Stephan Trüby, "5 Codes. Über Architektur, Paranoia und Risiko," in *5 Codes. Architektur, Paranoia und Risiko in Zeiten des Terrors*, ed. by Gerd de Bruyn, et. al. (IGMADE), Basel, Boston, Berlin, 2006, p. 17f.; since various ways of writing the term exist, the English word "code" will be used throughout the following essay. The German version, "Kode" will appear occasionally in the quotes.

2 Umberto Eco defines "code" as follows: "It establishes the rules for correlating expressive elements into content elements, after it first organizes both levels into a formal system or has taken on the previously organized forms of other codes. [...] A code only exists if there is a conventionalized and socialized correspondence, yet to which binding forces, extent, and timeframe it applies is unimportant." From Umberto Eco, *Segno*, Milan 1973. (Translation: Laura Bruce)

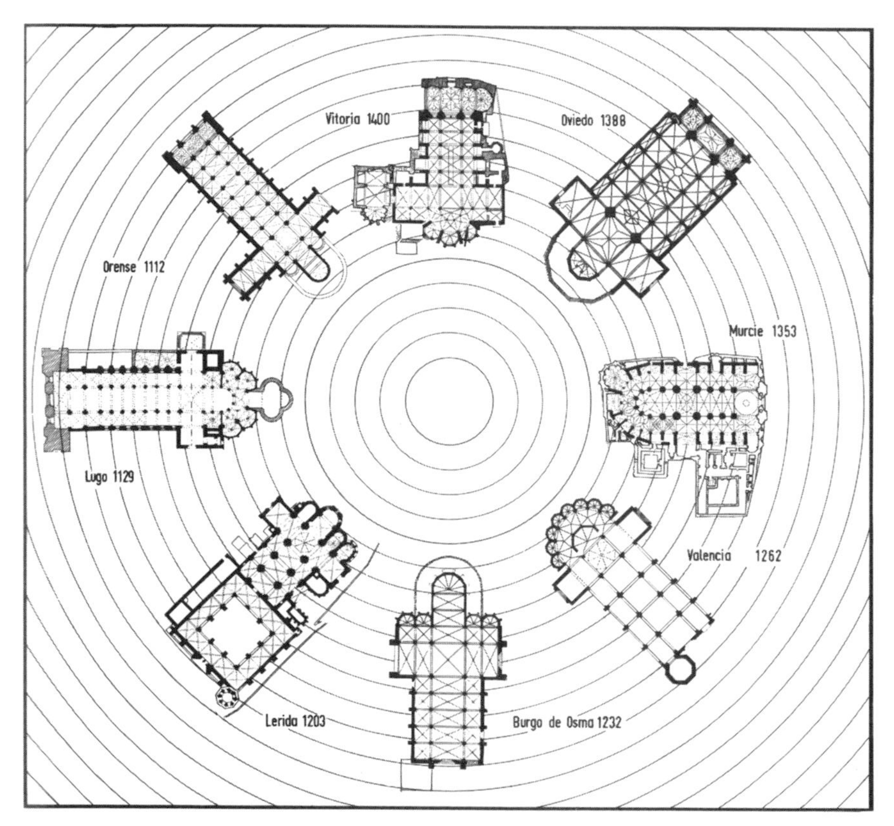

Fig. 1: Iconological symbolic code – 12–14th century Spanish cathedrals, diagram by Jencks and Baird, 1970.

historical, regional, typological, medial codes, and so on. Since there is still neither a unified definition nor a consistent terminology,[3] the following will attempt to outline some of the most important stations of the application of the code concept in the new semiotic-oriented architectural theory before shifting the focus to the situation today.[4]

The term "code" appeared regularly in the 1960s in the discussion about the relationship between modern architecture and information theory. The term was adopted from general communication theory and conveyed to architecture. The topic was taken up very early by Italian and French theorists and pursued using different approaches. One of these theorists was Gillo Dorfles, who speaks of an "iconographic code" in 1967, if a building is erected on the foundation of a "stationary, institutionalized semanticity."[5] He sees different codes of this sort applied in various historical sacred building types (pyramids, Greek temples, basilicas, mosques, and so on), where meanings determined by a set of definite formal principles are represented in new variations again and again. Dorfles only sees such "symbolic, iconographic" codes as being valid only for certain architectural projects and historical periods of architecture (as above with the sacred buildings in various cultures and epochs). In contemporary architecture, Dorfles recognizes "symbolic, iconographic" codes that are often used by the designing architects unintentionally and unknowingly because of habit, tradition, and standardization, and can therefore only be evaluated during an analysis. Identifying codes has a more critical or epistemological function, it is not suitable for practical orientation [Fig. 1].

3 On the semiotic debate about the code concept see Winfried Nöth, *Handbuch der Semiotik*, 2nd ed., Stuttgart, 2000, p. 216ff.; Gavin T. Watts and William C. Watts give a comprehensive overview in "Codes," as well as Rudi Keller and Helmut Lüdtke in "Kodewandel," in *Semiotik. Ein Handbuch zu den zeichentheoretischen Grundlagen von Natur und Kultur/Semiotics.* A Handbook on the Sign-Theoretic Foundations of Nature and Culture, ed. by Roland Posner et. al., vol. 1, Berlin, New York, 1997, pp. 414–435.

4 See here Claus Dreyer, "Semiotische Aspekte der Architekturwissenschaft: Architektursemiotik," in Posner, see note 3, vol. 3, 2003, pp. 3234–3278, p. 3256ff.

5 Gillo Dorfles, "Ikonologie und Semiotik in der Architektur," in *Architektur als Zeichensystem*, ed. by Alessandro Carlini and Bernhard Schneider, Tübingen, 1971, pp. 91–98, here: p. 97; a broader overview on the architectural-semiotic discourse of the 1960s can be found in Claus Dreyer, "Semiotik und Ästhetik in der Architekturtheorie der sechziger Jahre," in *Kulturtechnik Entwerfen. Praktiken, Konzepte und Medien in Architektur und Design Science*, ed. by Daniel Gethmann and Susanne Hauser, Bielefeld, 2009, pp. 179–201, here: p. 179ff.

In contrast, Umberto Eco also looked at the pragmatic side of architectural codes and developed many preliminary ideas from the Italian discussion.[6] Eco assumes that architecture plays an important role as a vehicle in a process of cultural communication: "Significant forms; codes that are compiled from the derivatives of habits, presented as structural models of given communication relationships; denotative and connotative signifieds that can be applied to the signifiers on the basis of code: this is the semiotic universe in which a communicative reading of architecture can process rigorously."[7] According to Eco, the architectural denotation refers mainly to the purpose and function of a building ("first function"), the architectural connotation to the type of concept and the interpretation or the "ideology" of the purpose and function ("second function").

These terms allow Eco to examine architectural codes more closely. He first differentiates between the "design code," which is the presentation and development of the architectural plan, and the "construction code" needed for realizing the architectural object. Both codes contain an "application" and a "reading" section – the latter being a precondition for the description and analysis of architectural objects, also for the viewer and critic. "Syntactic codes" affect the standard rules and regulations of construction elements and construction design such as wall, ceiling, column, beam, panels, structural frames, arches, and vaults: "There is no reference to function in these cases, nor to a denoted room, these contain purely a structural logic: they are the structural preconditions for the denotation of space."[8]

The "semantic codes" can be divided into two separate categories: The first is the articulation of architectural elements: those that denote "primary functions" such as the ceiling, window, stairs, terrace, wall; elements that connote "symbolic secondary functions" such as gable, column, cupola, tympanum; and ultimately elements that denote spatial programs and connote "ideologies of residential living" such as the dining room, living room, entrance hall, and common room. The second category is the articulation of typological genres that define "social types" such as villa, apartment house,

6 Umberto Eco, *La struttura assente*, Milan, 1968. (Translation: Laura Bruce)
7 Ibid.
8 Ibid.

train station, hospital, school, church, or "spatial types" such as labyrinth, open ground plan, central building, rotunda, hall, and so on.[9]

According to Eco, semantic codes refer particularly to invariants of the function and stereotypical patterns of use that are related to the organization of certain areas and functions; they also point to conventional and traditional types of use and appropriation. Due to restrictions such as these, Eco believes that architecture's potential for innovative and behavior-modifying design is very limited. He considers architecture to be more of a service than an art that can satisfy a social need within the framework of familiar and predictable solutions. "The codes being discussed were nothing more than iconographic, stylistic, or rhetorical encyclopedia. They do not offer any generative possibilities, but rather schemata, not open forms that can be discussed, but solidified forms, general relationships of an unexpected kind. Architecture is therefore rhetoric [...]",[10] that means it works with fixed, codified solutions that only have to be recombined and modified so as to give its users the impression that their needs have been fulfilled by means of architectural measures. Eco sees here a relationship between architecture and mass communication, and considers the "language of architecture" as being suasive and placating. It is ubiquitous and subliminal; it is subjected to fast changes in meaning and rash deterioration, it moves "between maximum coercion (you must live this way) and maximum lack of responsibility (you can use this form as you wish)"[11] and thus functions as any other product in a mass consumer society. Amid all this skepticism, Eco concludes that architecture has to go beyond the borders of its own codes in order to meet the demands of social and cultural change. "The architect must design variable primary functions and open secondary functions."[12] Semiotics can help by making people more aware of the methods and effectiveness of different architectural codes; it can also make it easier for practicing architects to go beyond or deconstruct traditional codes, and even discover new codes (which would become an objective of postmodernism, see below) [Fig. 2].

9 Ibid.
10 Ibid.
11 Ibid.
12 Ibid.

Fig. 2: Rhetorical code – Charles Moore: *Piazza d'Italia*, New Orleans, 1976–1979.

It can be said that Charles Jencks introduced and popularized this idea of going beyond the limits in his analysis entitled *The Language of Post-Modern Architecture*[13] and, hence, also triggered a wide-reaching paradigm shift in architectural communication: instead of function (or at least in addition to it), it is now also possible to communicate "fictions" and represent them architecturally.[14] This requires specific codes that architects can use to make their buildings significant signs (or sign complexes). These codes, which were not defined more precisely but illustrated and described in many examples, can be interpreted as "sub-languages" with a limited inventory of signs and that do not need to be sharply differentiated from one another: he presented codes that are traditionalist, avant-garde, technological, natural language code, regionalist, commercial, historicist, as well as other codes. Jencks placed special value on codes that could be perceived and interpreted as metaphors, because they generate associative references to non-architectural realms, for example through anthropomorphic or organic forms.[15]

Jencks believes this type of architectural communication to be particularly appropriate in a pluralistic and multicultural society. He therefore calls for a "double coding"[16] system as a basic principle for postmodern architecture that can express the architectural message by using first avant-garde and elite codes that are familiar to experts and insiders, as well as conventional and popular codes known by the average user and other relevant people, so as to allow the message to be interpreted from different perspectives.

The "elite code" largely refers to historical architecture in general, to the classic modernism specifically, as well as to contemporary art and culture and the aesthetic standards of the relevant theories; it can be adopted and made available only through education and extensive training, and is consequently very common among the academic and professional areas of architectural production and reception.

13 Charles Jencks, *The Language of Post-Modern Architecture*, London, 1977.

14 This hypothesis was first explicitly represented by Heinrich Klotz in 1984, yet it was intellectually anticipated in 1977 by Jencks. See note 13 and Heinrich Klotz, *The History of Postmodern Architecture* (1984), Cambridge/Mass., 1988.

15 See for example the metaphorical interpretations of Le Corbusiers' chapel in Ronchamp by Jencks, see note 13, p. 57.

16 Charles Jencks, "Post-Modern History," in *Architectural Design* 1 (1978), pp. 11–58, here: p.13ff.

Fig. 3: Eclectic code – Charles Jencks, Terry Farrell: *Thematic House,* living room, London, 1984.

In contrast, the "popular code" refers to the everyday world of the "average user," to their conventions and practical schemas for comfortable architecture, to the paragons from fashion, advertising, and media, as well as to the aesthetic standards of pop culture. As everyday experience, it is part of most people's basic equipment today and, hence, is subject to a certain level of expectation. Jencks perceives "radical eclecticism" or "adhocism" in architecture as an ideal realization of this concept, which mixes heterogeneous elements to form a creative synthesis, so as to offer a pluralistic society as many interpretations as possible. In a type of "anything goes!" enthusiasm, postmodern architecture made good use of this recipe, even occasionally giving rhetorical arbitrariness so much free rein that it resulted in complete confusion. Nevertheless, this approach stimulated the "re-semiotizing" of architecture in the 1970s and 1980s [Fig. 3].

The universal phenomenon of postmodernism, which pervaded western culture's every nook and cranny,[17] affected architecture by triggering since the 1970s a comprehensive transformation in outward appearance that can be described as a practical research on the semiotics of the built form.[18] It redefined, in particular, the roles and potential of classic and contemporary architectural codes. Some evident aspects are the re-emergence of historical and typological forms; the integration of regional, contextual, and situative elements; the mixing of popular and elite, "familiar" and "foreign" or exotic means of expression; the "staged" arrangement and ironic estrangement; fragmentation and diversification as well as fictionalization and "poetization." The predominant methods of realizing this transformation are illustrating, quoting, copying, montage, trivialization, and theatralization.[19] Moreover, all these

17 See Jürgen Habermas, *The Philosophical Discourse of Modernity. Twelve Lectures* (1985), Cambridge/Mass., 1987; Andreas Huyssen and Klaus Scherpe (eds.), *Postmoderne. Zeichen eines kulturellen Wandels,* Reinbek, 1986; Wolfgang Welsch, *Unsere postmoderne Moderne,* 2nd rev. ed., Weinheim, 1988.

18 See note 14, as well as Jürgen Habermas, "Modern and Postmodern Architecture" (1985), in J. Habermas, *The New Conservatism. Cultural Criticism and the Historians' Debate,* ed. and transl. by Shierry W. Nicholsen, Cambridge/Mass., 1989.

19 See Claus Dreyer, "The Performance of Space in Recent Architecture," in *Signs of Humanity – L'homme et ses signes,* ed. by Michael Balat and Janice Delledale-Rhodes, Berlin, New York, 1992, vol. 2, pp. 949–961, and Claus Dreyer: "Zitat und Zitieren in zeitgenössischer Architektur," in *Zeitschrift für Semiotik,* 14/1–2 (1992), pp. 41–59.

methods do in fact deal with the process of coding as interpreted by Eco and Jencks as described above. Both the emergence of the individual form and the accompanying forming processes obviously refer to the possible meanings which may be attributed to them: for example, the direct reference to historical forms (such as Charles Moores *Piazza d'Italia* in New Orleans, 1977–78, see Fig. 2), or the reference to artistic and exotic paragons (such as Hans Hollein's *Österreichisches Verkehrsbüro* in Vienna, 1976–78, now destroyed), through the metaphorical over-glorification of typological motifs (like Charles Jencks and Terry Farrell's *Thematic House* in London, 1979–84, see Fig. 3), the formalistic stylization of geometric patterns (such as Oswald Mathias Ungers' *Deutsches Architekturmuseum* in Frankfurt am Main, 1979–84), or the "historical estrangement" of classical themes (such as Michael Graves' *Portland Building* in Portland, Oregon, 1980–82).[20] The different types of references to meanings by using different codes can be analyzed and characterized more precisely in each specific instance, in order to provide interpretations.[21] Yet, this approach requires that architects redefine architectural codes while bearing in mind that old and conventional signs can be fulfilled and combined with more contemporary statements. They cannot and should not be, according to the fundamental self-image and historical view, one-dimensional, clear, and consistent messages; they should rather be assembled pluralistically, and be ambiguous, "double coded," but capable of entering a dialog in order to meet the demands of the times.

Wolfgang Welsch studied the role of architectural codes in postmodern architecture in depth.[22] He uses the words "code," "language," and occasionally "style" in his analysis to a large extent as synonyms, which can be explained by his focus on architecture's communicative capacity in a pluralistic culture.[23]

Welsch considered James Stirling's *Neue Staatsgalerie* in Stuttgart (1978–84, see Fig. 4), a "parade example of explicit multilingualism" that displays numerous characteristics of "double or multi-coding." According to Welsch's

20 See the related illustrations and other examples in Klotz, see note 14.

21 On the significance of the determining codes for the purpose of analyzing and interpreting architecture see Claus Dreyer, "Interpretation von Architektur als semiotisches Programm. Zu Gregor Schneiders 'Cube' in Hamburg 2007," *in Wolkenkuckucksheim* 1 (2008).

22 Welsch, see note 17, p. 87ff.

23 Ibid., p. 20.

extensive analysis, Stirling's building can be interpreted so as to bring forward how "his construction is [...] blatantly multilingual"[24] and how it is not just an example of "mixing styles, but rather relates contemporary world styles and forms of life."[25]

The coherence of the divergences is an important point in Welsch's plea for the performance of different codes in architectural design: despite the many contrasts, there have to be connections that lead to a, perhaps even fragile, unity and thus allow for communication.[26] There is no patent recipe that creates the ability for dialog, but rather a "factual success should be found and assessed in each individual example."[27]

It is obvious that Welsch takes as a basis an extremely broad understanding of language and code in architecture: one could say that it is really about a formal vocabulary derived from extremely varied sources, and interconnected and composed into a complex whole according to an artistic logic and grammar, and which can only be deciphered and interpreted in an elaborate and complex analysis with immense expert knowledge. What remains is the impression of very elite architectural coding that completely disregards the popular counterpart championed by Jencks. This is not a disadvantage to the success of the building as a museum, as was demonstrated in 2009 by the great public response to the twenty-fifth anniversary of the new *Stuttgart Staatsgalerie*. One could even insinuate a conventionalization and popularization of the elite code by use and familiarization, something that, in fact, could be considered a successful communication strategy.

The worldwide success of postmodern architecture and the great rise in the popularity of the code strategy – particularly in consumer, event, and prefabricated architecture – led to widespread criticism of "ubiquitous application design"[28] and its nice columns, pretty gables, little towers, and ornaments, which effectively discredited the concept and practice of architectural coding. "Code" and

24 Ibid., p. 21.
25 Ibid., p. 117f.
26 Ibid., p. 119.
27 Ibid., p. 120.
28 Hubertus Adam, "Zwischen Banalität und Extravaganz. Postmoderne Architektur – und ihre (Nach)Wirkungen," in *Die Revision der Postmoderne,* exhibition catalog Deutsches Architekturmuseum Frankfurt, ed. by Ingeborg Flagge and Romana Schneider, Hamburg, 2004, pp. 62–73, here: p. 63.

Fig. 4: Plural coding – James Stirling: *Neue Staatsgalerie Stuttgart*, 1977–1984.

"postmodern" became swear words that tainted any and all attempts to apply explicitly formal language in architectural design. This situation ultimately led to a return to a fundamental, abstract, and "eternal" architectural language,[29] while provoking the emergence of a neohistorical and reconstructive form of architecture that takes a deliberate stand against criticism from the elite and is very popular among the general public.[30] However, this does not resolve the code and coding issue from a semiotic perspective, because it was never fixed to specific individual codes in the first place. It was, instead, always viewed and applied as a methodical instrumentarium for the analysis and interpretation of many different sign systems that can be identified as limited sign processes in relation to larger sign processes (postmodernism just happened to be a particularly suitable and willing field of application). The code's repertoire of signs, and above all their meanings, has changed, yet "coding strategies" in architectural design are also under the influence of digital media and have changed drastically. The two authors mentioned in detail above, Jencks and Welsch, have only recently begun reviewing earlier works and attempting to redefine their positions.

Welsch asserted a new semantic orientation of architectural codes in contemporary environmental designs, which also requires and already generates a new repertory of signs. He wanted to observe a shift from the anthropocentric, artificial, and elite high culture coding towards a more natural, organic, and cosmological formal language, which leads to "transhuman" design and emphasizes the "fundamental *Weltzugehörigkeit*"[31] of humans. "The city should not be conceived as a space solely for humans – because this is the only way it can allow human existence to fully unfold in all possible dimensions. To be precise, we should think and plan from the outside in and not from the inside out. The transhuman aspects should not be brought forth retrospectively, but should play a vital role in determining the form from the very beginning."[32] Welsch also sees examples of this new coding in computer-generated designs, in which "biomorphic architectural ideas take root, [...] which are looking for a means of designing that

29 See Oswald Mathias Ungers, "Wir stehen am Anfang," in ibid., pp. 108–119, here: p. 108ff.

30 See Werner Sewing, *Bildregie. Architektur zwischen Retrodesign und Eventkultur,* Basel, Boston, Berlin, 2003.

31 Wolfgang Welsch, "Was war die Postmoderne – und was könnte aus ihr werden?," in Flagge and Schneider, see note 28, pp. 32–39, here: p. 38.

32 Ibid.

Fig. 5: Biomorphic code – Peter Cook and Colin Fournier: *Kunsthaus Graz*, 2005.

takes our biological, motor, and sensorial existence better into account than decidedly rationalist architecture."[33] Plural codes would not only support the dialog between cultures, but would also integrate nature and the cosmos into the communicative universe [Fig. 5].

This approach was further developed by Jencks who, as Welsch, also pursued the concept of multi-coding but stressed it more as the emergence of new paradigms and, as a consequence, made a rather significant step towards speculation. Influenced by the theory of evolution, cosmology, and complexity theory, as well as the expanding possibilities of computer programs, the "fold" or the "blob" (in effect "drops") create new basic forms that add to the diversity of architectural codes and give expression to a new understanding of the world. After explicitly formal codes had been discredited, these abstract forms allow for a rather "allusive symbolism"[34] that, following the disappearance of the "great narrative," challenges open interpretations against the background of contemporary experience. Various forms and motifs can be recognized and interpreted from different variations of the code that remain abstract and open or, in connection with explicit signs, can evoke obvious interpretations. This would have still have done justice to the old concept of mixing popular and elite codes.

Jencks considers Frank O. Gehry's *Guggenheim Museum* (1997) in Bilbao an example of a successful realization of the varied fold principle, because it "represents both the flowing, folding, and movement that is typical of the fold theory, as well as the self-organized systems and fractal orders of the complexity theory."[35] [Fig. 6] The multifarious coding in this building allows for a unique order to develop. Moreover, a homogenous whole emerges despite the difference of the individual parts and segments because, as Jencks emphasizes, of the masterly use of computer programs during the design phase: according to the principle of "self-similarity," they allow difference to develop from unity and unity to develop from the difference of the original code.[36] This is also decisive for the concept of

33 Ibid., p. 39.
34 Charles Jencks, "The Post-Modern Metanarrative," in Flagge and Schneider, see note 28, pp. 12–31, here: p. 22.
35 Ibid., p. 24. See also my attempt to read and interpret the building in Claus Dreyer, "Über das Interpretieren von Architektur," in *Architektur – Sprache. Buchstäblichkeit, Versprachlichung, Interpretation,* ed. by Eduard Führ, Hans Friesen, and Anette Sommer, Munich, 1998, pp. 33–48.
36 See note 34, p. 25.

Fig. 6: Abstract code ("folding") – Frank Gehry: *Guggenheim Museum*, Bilbao, 1993–1997.

"blobs" that embody a different versatile coding in contemporary architectural design. These are regular or irregular, multi-curvate forms similar to biomorphic and organic shapes and also suggestive of cosmological models. Jencks calls the products of this code (and those of the fold's) "enigmatic signifiers"[37] (which could be translated as "curious signs") that are rooted in the paradigm of complexity and capable of creating highly expressive, meaningful, sculptural, and iconic architecture. Jencks singles out the *Swiss Re Tower* in London by Sir Norman Foster as an example for this type of coding [Fig. 7].

Jencks and Welsch before him had no doubt that the meaning of the new codes (with the paradigms "fold" and "blob") could refer to the history of the universe, to cosmology, as well as the evolution and complexity theory, and integrate with the help of the "computer production of individualized elements [...] a series of expressive means approximating nature (for example fractal grammars, strange or chaotic attractors, fluid morphologies, and so on)."[38] It is clear that these new codes first have to develop, differentiate, conventionalize, and become embedded into architectural practice, but it is absolutely certain that contemporary architecture can no longer be imagined without the program of "verbalization," mediatization, and multi-coding.

This is evident in the computer-generated architectural designs and projects that have become more and more visible recently. Their emergence is the result of complex computer program applications and their underlying program codes. Here, the codes are rules that are formulated in specific "languages" and which determine, often algorithmically, how the project-specific data is to be processed. In these programs, the meanings of the coded signs largely relate to the programmed structures that are, for example, defined by logic or mathematics. Consequently, from a semiotic point of view, it is possible to speak mainly of "syntactic codes." As a result, great freedom can be discovered in the design, which in turn can create, for a given data basis, a large number of programmable formal structures that might be considered possible solutions for spatial configurations. The "semantic codes" of modern and postmodern architecture, as well as a good measure of intuition, can be used again during the selection and decision process for the final results of these development processes. They could even possess a

37 Ibid.
38 Ibid., p. 30.

Fig. 7: Enigmatic Code ("blob") – Norman Foster: *Swiss Re – Headquarters*, London, 2001–2003.

cultural anchor not only for the reading and interpreting, but also for the creative application.

From a semiotic perspective, architectural codes alert us to the fact that the conception and production of architecture is always linked to a process of coding that can be implemented in the design, as well as in the responses and interpretation. In the broadest sense, it is even possible to say that un-coded architecture does not exist.[39] Architectural codes are multifaceted, complex, diverse, and defined in very different levels of clarity. They sometimes have the status of formal "languages" (of the stylistic or geometric kind), sometimes they create incomplete or even completely open relationships by having signifiers without clear signifieds (Jencks' "enigmatic signifiers"), and they are often a mixture of both. The pictorial ("iconic") and symbolic ("semantic") codes of historical and postmodern architecture compete with the abstract ("syntactic") codes of geometry, mathematics, and digital programs, which are applied and often combined in classic modernism or in "fold" and "blob" architecture. The description and analysis, as well as the creative use of codes demands a certain level of professionalism that has to be first acquired. There will always be misunderstandings, perplexity, and misconstructions, yet these are far outweighed by the potential for open and new interpretations of undefined or complex signs. Many architectural codes are culturally or socially anchored and are acquired and conveyed via customs and education. Architectural codes have a long tradition and history (and if historical styles are added to the codes, this history is very long) and are subject to constant change that can, at times, lead to disappearance. But new codes are always being created from cultural, technical, and social developments. They are the expression for an innovative and advanced world- and self-conception of the particular age. Architectural semiotics attempts to describe and interpret these developments and, thus, contribute to a better understanding of our cultural orientation in the built environment.

39 See Ingeborg M. Rocker, "When Code Matters," in *Architectural Digest*, 76/421 (2006), p. 21.

Georg Vrachliotis

GROPIUS' QUESTION OR ON REVEALING AND CONCEALING CODE IN ARCHITECTURE AND ART

"Will it [...] be necessary to educate a new profession of architectural assistants for the purpose of articulating the problems to be solved into the proper language of the computer?"[1] Walter Gropius, Bauhaus founder and one of the most famous architects of the twentieth century posed this question to the audience at the *First Boston Conference on Architecture and the Computer.* It addressed a topic that was on the minds of many architects present in the ballroom of the distinguished Sheraton Plaza Hotel. The audience was curious, but not only because such a renowned figure was invited to speak at the first architecture conference on the topic of the computer – Gropius was in the middle of planning the satellite city named after him in Berlin, and eighty-one at the time, meaning he was also the oldest speaker at the historical symposium. Hence, this was the first time that the potential and limits of the computer in architecture were discussed on such a distinguished level.

H. Morse Payne, president of the Boston Architectural Center and an assistant of Walter Gropius, welcomed the audience with the following words: "Our topic, the computer, seems the most timely, the most urgent, the most serious subject that we could bring to the profession."[2] He went on to diagnose the profession as "steeped in time-honored traditional methods of approaching architectural assignments, but this machine, a product of our day and our time, might require us to change and approach our task in some new manner. So, we must begin to explore the subject immediately."[3] Payne's short introductory speech was more than a challenge to the architects present – it had the character of a public appeal directed at architecture as an entire discipline. It was time to finally hop on the bandwagon of technical progress and begin researching the computer and its potential for architecture.[4]

1 Walter Gropius, "Computers for Architectural Design," in *Architecture and the Computer. Proceedings of the First Boston Architectural Center Conference* (Boston: Boston Architectural Center at MIT, December 5, 1964), from the department of architecture, MIT, p. 41.

2 H. Morse Payne, "Welcome," in ibid., p. 1.

3 Payne, ibid.

4 Payne, ibid.

Yet no one was really sure just how to approach these new machines, despite the pioneer spirit Payne was trying to arouse at the architectural center that evening. Technologically speaking, the computer was completely new ground for architects at the beginning of the 1960s, and was mostly seen as an artifact by technicians for technicians – except in large planning and construction firms, where it was already being applied as an administrative calculating machine. However, the actual thought of drawing or even entering into a "dialog" with computers must have sounded like the beginnings of a remote, futuristic architectural practice. Most architects could not even fathom how or where computers might be integrated into their practice's diverse creative design and planning processes – and any ideas of what a computer actually was or even looked like were mainly derived from photographs of massive mainframe computers bathed in cold, bright light and stylized to represent the sober, rational world of applied mathematics. It was an unfamiliar world of codes and programs, but with a mysterious and seductive sheen that was nevertheless mesmerizing.

An architect could not imagine ever being able to operate a computer in the design process, let alone program it – not only because they lacked the knowledge, but also because (and for many this was the true reason) they did not feel that using computers was part of a designing architect's job. Two separate worlds were colliding here: the creative and intuitive designing universalist, and the performative technician who also happened to hold the knowledge about this new world. So, what would Payne's suggestion to explore the computer as an architectural tool actually look like? The hands-on, manual operation of computers was delegated to engineers or the administrative areas of construction planning. Which is why the skeptical question "[B]ut what about us, the designers?"[5] was raised in Boston.

Gropius' answer was short and sweet. "Still I believe, if we look at those machines as potential tools to shorten our working processes, they might help us to free our creative power."[6] Believing that the machine could shorten the working process and liberate creativity was – or, better said, is – a widespread attitude in architecture. However, the most interesting aspect for this discus-

5 Natalie Jaffe, "Architects Weigh Computer's Uses," *New York Times* (December 6, 1964).

6 Jaffe, ibid.

sion lies in Gropius' question at the start of this essay. He was talking about a "proper language of the computer" and the "architectural assistant." In order to apply the computer to the field of architecture in a useful manner, a translator was required that knew the language of both the computer and architecture. If architects were ready to consider computers as a viable architectural tool, as Payne calls for in his introductory speech, it would be necessary to assign a decisive function to Gropius' idea of the architectural assistant. Almost four decades later, and in view of increasingly complex computer programs, it is also important to discuss whether architecture is still a field consisting of specialists, translators, and architectural assistants – or whether the now largely university-engendered profession of architects, who have become algorithm-designers themselves, may be taking the lead. It seems we still owe Gropius an answer.

About Drawing as Gesture

Drawing has historically been considered a fundamental medium for architects and engineers. The architect uses drawing in the form of sketches, ground plans, perspective views, and for presentation and design, so as to give form to the abstract contours in his or her imaginary world – yet, far more importantly, the act of drawing is also a means of intersubjectively visualizing the media-related traces of one's own thoughts. "Geometry and line"[7] can articulate, communicate, and intensify knowledge contained inside the mind. In terms of an instrument, drawing is related to writing – regarding the free movement of the hand, the consolidation of one's own thoughts, or the individual character of one's handwriting.[8] The act of drawing is a gesture in Vilém Flusser's terms, who conceptualizes writing as a gesture.[9] Flusser very roughly defines gesture as primarily "a movement of the body or of the tool connected to it, for which there is no satisfactory casual explanation."[10] Writing and drawing are closely

7 Werner Oechslin, "Geometrie und Linie. Die Vitruvianische 'Wissenschaft' von der Architekturzeichnung," *Daidalos* 1 (1981), p. 20ff. See also Winfried Nerdinger (ed.), *Die Architekturzeichnung. Vom barocken Idealplan zur Axonometrie. Zeichnungen aus der Architektursammlung der Technischen Universität München,* exhibition catalog Deutsches Architekturmuseum Frankfurt, Munich, 1987.

8 See Walter Koschatzky, *Die Kunst der Zeichnung: Technik, Geschichte, Meisterwerke,* Munich, 1999.

9 See Vilém Flusser, *Gesten. Versuch einer Phänomenologie,* Frankfurt am Main, 1997, pp. 32–41.

10 Flusser, ibid., p. 8.

related. They are both a "phenomenolization of the thought process."[11] First, the algorithmization of the drawing process, which began in the age of cybernetics, triggered a ripple of conceptual and methodical uncertainty throughout the field of architecture, which then changed architectural drawing as a genre, and even more, architecture as a discipline. The intuitive dialog between the performative hand and the creative eye was severely damaged, for one, because when the computer arrived, the traditional idea of the connection between drawing and seeing, and also of drawing as seeing, was subject to scrutiny by a new technical knowledge and the associated operational criteria.[12]

The Hidden Code: Drawing Instead of Programming

Only a few years after the historical conference in Boston, a young architect by the name of Nicholas Negroponte founded the *Architecture Machine Group.* It was the first center for architectural computer research and later renamed *Media Lab,* almost as though he was taking Gropius and Payne literally. It immediately calls to mind photos of architects in checked shirts surrounded by circuits and drawing plotters, concentrating on the slightly curved glass surfaces of their small computer monitors. They drew simple line drawings or assembled them using a collection of prepared drawing elements, looking very serious while doing so, on computers that would be unbelievably expensive for today's standards. The serious treatment of these machines was – and this has not changed much apparently – an attempt to develop tools for the architectural production of tomorrow: "imagine an architect [...] seated at a computer console of the future."[13] A sequence of images in Negroponte's book about the *Architecture Machine Group* demonstrates the difficulty involved in this task. They show the hands of a man sitting in front of a typewriter-like machine gesticulating while trying to operate it [Fig. 1]. The caption states: "In these few seconds the user of this terminal has said more to the machine in hand-movement language than in any string of text, but it is all unheard. This particular

11 Flusser, ibid., p. 35.

12 See Georg Vrachliotis, *Geregelte Verhältnisse. Architektur und technisches Denken in der Epoche der Kybernetik,* Vienna, New York (forthcoming in 2010).

13 Steve A. Coons, "Computer Aided Design," in *Architecture and the Computer. Proceedings of the First Boston Architectural Center Conference* (Boston: Boston Architectural Center at MIT, December 5, 1964), from the department of architecture, MIT, p. 26.

person has never used a machine before; he does not know what a language is without gestures."[14] The last statement, "a language without gesture," is particularly interesting in relation to Flusser. It is easy to describe writing as a gesture, which is clearly seen in the sequence of images. Yet it is worth noting that Negroponte interprets working with computer code as using a language without gesture. Here, he identifies a hurdle that we are still trying to overcome in architecture: programming, in other words, working with code, in contrast to drawing, is an undertaking without gesture.

The mathematician Ivan Sutherland, a Ph.D. student of Claude Shannon, was also aware of this hurdle while he developed between 1961 and 1963 a revolutionary computer graphic program, which he called *Sketchpad*[15]. Sutherland believed a user should be able to operate a computer on a visual basis, and not only on a mathematical and logical basis. The program codes for machine commands, which originally were only in written form, were supplemented and replaced in *Sketchpad* by "drawn" commands. Negroponte's "language without gesture" became a "language with gesture": it became drawing. Sutherland utilized a new technology called "light pen," developed by military radar research, which made it possible to "draw" directly onto the monitor and change the drawing on various levels.

Two years after Sutherland launched his program, mathematician Douglas C. Engelbart developed the "pointing device," an innovative, optical input tool that replaced the light pen that was used to draw directly onto the monitor. It was initially a small, manually maneuvered wooden box, which would later become known as first the "optical mouse" and, ultimately, the "computer mouse." Architects took to Englebart's invention very quickly [Fig. 2]. In 1968, some years later, architect David Evans introduced Englebart's invention at the *First International Conference on Architecture and Computer Graphics.*[16] It showed that an architect could create and change a drawing much more elegantly and precisely with this tool than with the awkward pencil that was

14 Nicholas Negroponte, *The Architecture Machine Group,* Cambridge/Mass., 1970, p. 13.
15 Ivan E. Sutherland, *Sketchpad. A man-machine graphical communication system,* Lincoln Laboratory Technical Report no. 296, Massachusetts Institute of Technology, January 1963.
16 See David Evans, "Augmented Human Intellect," in *Computer Graphics in Architecture and Design. Proceedings of the Yale Conference on Architecture and Computer Graphics,* (April 1968), ed. by Murray Milne, New Haven, 1969, p. 62ff.

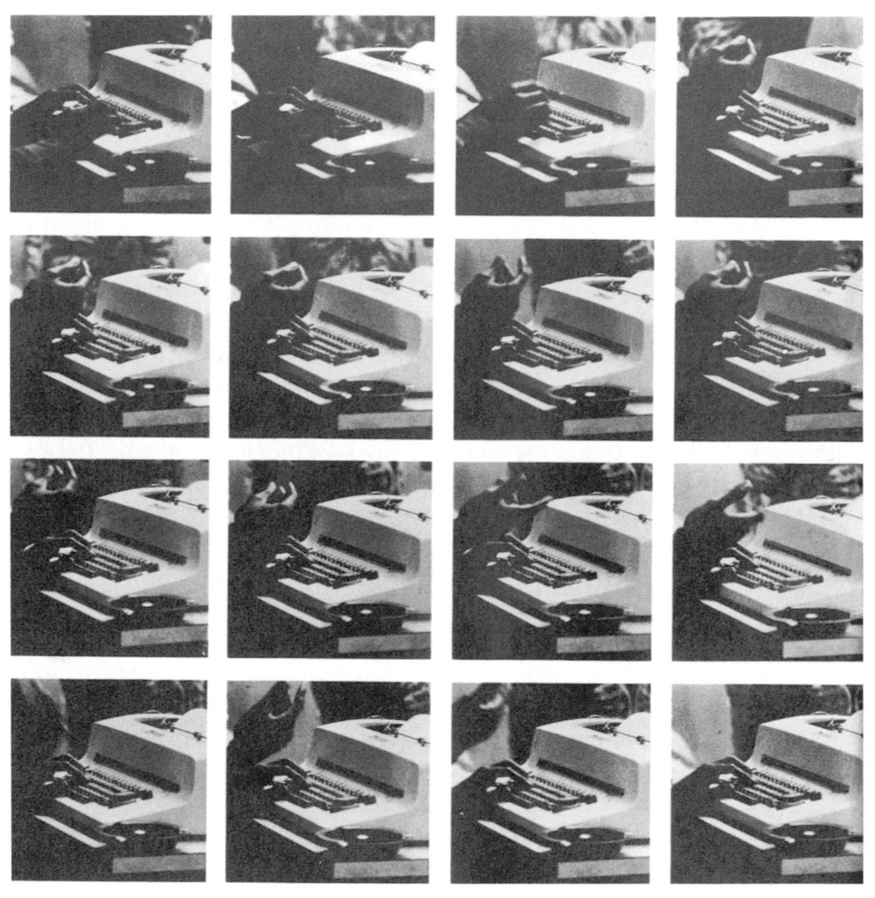

Fig. 1: Image series from *The Architecture Machine*, 1970.

attached to a cable and had to be used directly on the monitor. "If the use of computers by architects is inevitable, then, clearly the problem must be faced of how architects are to 'talk' to the computers."[17] This articulates one of the core challenges at the *Computer Graphics in Architecture and Design* conference at Yale in 1968. Steve Coons, computer pioneer und mentor to the young Negroponte, stated confidently that "[n]o architect wants to become or should want to become an expert computer programmer. Architects want to do architecture. City planners want to do city planning. They don't want to have to invent and manufacture the pencils they use. They want to have them at hand. The computer is a tool. We want to arrange matters so that the computer can be used as naturally and easily as a pencil [...]."[18] As could be expected, this statement was met with great approval by the architectural profession, in view of the fact that architects above all were traditionally considered designers who used drawing to communicate their ideas. According to Coons' concept of technology, it was the new technology that had to change to meet the needs of designing architects, and not the architects who had to adapt to their tools. They should not have to learn, bearing Negroponte in mind, the "language without gesture."

The Revealed Code: Programming Instead of Drawing

During the "tool building" trend in America, an artistic and philosophical branch of computer graphics was being developed in postwar Europe that differed from Coon's and Negroponte's approaches in various ways. Computer graphics were being programmed and not "drawn." The productive twilight of cybernetics, art, and philosophy led to an experimental programming culture that would spawn a completely new artistic type.[19] The three central figures of this code culture were the two young mathematicians Frieder Nake and Georg

17 *Computer Graphics and Architecture. Program Statement: On the Relevance of Computer Processes, specially Computer Graphics, to Architecture.* Unpublished document, Warren McCulloch Archive, American Philosophical Society.

18 Steve A. Coons, "Computer Aided Design," in *Computer Graphics in Architecture and Design,* see note 15, p. 9.

19 See Frieder Nake, "Informatik als Gestaltungswissenschaft: Eine Herausforderung an das Design," in *Algorithmik, Kunst, Semiotik. Hommage für Frieder Nake,* ed. by Karl-Heinz Rödinger, Heidelberg, 2003, pp. 142–165.

Fig. 2: Image series from *The Architecture Machine*, 1970 (collected and arranged by the author).

Nees, and their philosophical mentor Max Bense. Nake and Nees turned programming into a modern form of an aesthetic craft,[20] and Bense brought this craft to a new theoretical level. In the process, a close reciprocity developed between the aesthetic craft and the aesthetic theory: on the one hand, Nake's and Nees' line drawings seemed to contain traces of Bense's art theory. Yet on the other, many of Bense's essays could be read as philosophical decoding aids, which were imperative to understanding the abstract aesthetics of Nake's and Nees' programmed residual images and chance graphics. While playing on the machine, small drawings were created that displayed sometimes ordered, sometimes erratic and irregular patterns of seemingly chance clusterings, superimpositions, textures, and fine patterns, made from points, lines, or circles [Fig. 3]. Some of these machine drawings could be traced to an error in the programming, thus creating chance patterns. The visual results of the faulty program amazed the young mathematicians at the computer center. At the same time from an art theoretical perspective, it was clear that these small black and white drawings harbored an unimaginably explosive force.

Programming a drawing in this context entails thinking on the level of a machine code, regardless of what the drawing will represent, which program language will be used, or which system will be coded. Working on the level of computer codes means using machine logic.[21] A code consists here of symbolic signs and is nothing more than "text, basically text,"[22] as Nake himself emphasizes. The computer becomes a type of semiotic, technical artifact – or, in the words of the computer scientist Wolfgang Coy, a "semiotic machine."[23] Seen in this light, computer graphics could be interpreted as the aesthetic trail of a text, which is unique because it can be read from two perspectives: by humans, even if it involves a certain level of difficulty, and by machines as an operational code. Drawing with code means operating with text.

20 See Hans Dieter Hellige, "Zur Genese des informatischen Programmbegriffs: Begriffbildung, metaphorische Prozesse, Leitbilder und professionelle Kulturen," in: *Algorithmik, Kunst, Semiotik. Hommage für Frieder Nake,* ed. by Karl-Heinz Rödinger, Heidelberg, 2003, pp. 42–75.

21 See Gabriele Gramelsberger, in this book, pp. 29–40.

22 Frieder Nake, letter to the author, May 5, 2008.

23 Wolfgang Coy, "Aus der Vorgeschichte des Computers als Medium," in *Computer als Medium,* ed. by Norbert Bolz, Friedrich A. Kittler, and Christoph Tholen, Munich, 1994, p. 19.

22. Upheaval collection (a)
Stages of a star-form composed of a network of lines into a cube, by means of a random improvisation.
Idea by Masao Komura, programme by Junio Yamanaka (CTG)
23. Upheaval collection (b)
Further developments in the transformation of a two-dimensional star-form into a cube in perspective.
Idea by Masao Komura, programme by Kunio Yamanaka (CTG)
24. Hexagon involving cubes
The detail of the forms is established by random means.
Idea by Masao Komura, programme by Kunio Yamanaka (CTG)

Right, CTG Computer Poetry aims only at the effect of combining letters of the alphabet according to certain rules. Words and sentences are regarded only as a sequential development of the alphabet. The poetry is composed by using random procedures. Idea and programme by Haruki Tsuchiya (CTG), who writes: 'The poetry is hard to read at a glance. But if you read it you will find a wonderful experience in the unknown world of sound, word, language and letter.'

Notes on the programming of computer graphics

Frieder Nake

Computer graphics are diagrammatic forms, or figures, produced by means of a digital electronic computer and a drawing instrument which is either a direct component of the computer or connected to it, e.g. punch tape or magnetic band.

My first computer graphics were produced in Germany in December 1963 at the Computer Institute of the Stuttgart Polytechnic. Shortly afterwards, and independently, Georg Nees started making computer graphics in Erlangen.

In Stuttgart, I used the Graphomat Zuse Z 64 drawing machine controlled by punch tape. The machine has a drawing head guiding four pens, fed by Indian ink of different colours with nibs of varying thicknesses.

The production of computer graphics is a three-stage process:

1. setting up a programme for the computer;
2. automatic feeding of the programme into the computer;
3. automatic conversion of the information delivered. The latter is contained in a punch tape and is transposed by the drawing machine into the lines of the diagrammatic figures.

Rectangular hatchings by Frieder Nake

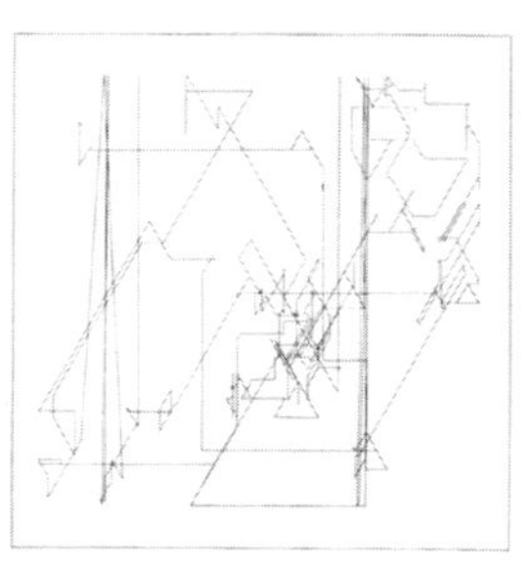

Computer graphic *Polygonal course No. 7*, 13.9.1965, random elements include:
1. number of polygonal angles
2. direction of each polygonal side
3. length of each polygonal side

The first and most important task is that of setting up a programme which should make it possible to produce an entire class of drawings ('aesthetic objects' as referred to by Max Bense) running through a specific pattern in all its variations. An analogy may be drawn here to the artistic process of pursuing a theme through all its possibilities guided by 'intuition'. Here the concept of 'intuition' refers to the choosing of possibilities from a given repertoire. The computer simulates intuition by the automatic selection of pseudo-random numbers.

It is best to explain the process with the programme used for producing a series of *Rectangular hatchings*; the common theme of these drawings is the spacing of horizontally or vertically shaded rectangles. For this purpose a programme was set up to produce a class of drawings consisting of rectangular-shaped hatchings parallel to the borders of the illustrations. Then all those elements of a drawing belonging to that class, which are arbitrary, must be determined. In this particular graphic the variable elements were;

1. N number of hatchings per illustration.
2. Position x y per hatching (i.e. determined by the position of the lower left-hand corner of the rectangle).

77

Fig. 3: Frieder Nake's contribution to the exhibition *Cybernetic Serendipity. The Computer and the Arts*, 1968 at the Institute of Contemporary Arts, London.

Nake's and Nees' first computer graphics shifted the emphasis from methodology to technology, giving the program theory a completely new twist. This was demonstrated very clearly by the *Computergrafik – Programme*[24] exhibition, which was organized as early as 1965 and where Nake and Nees showed some of their earlier works. However, they showed more than their graphics, they also presented the program code that accompanied it. In other words, they showed the structural source and not only the result. The picture hung next to its code, and the code next to its picture [Fig. 4]. The form, or the image, was separated from its structure, the code. Displaying a code in this way, like a work of art hanging on the wall, was more than a didactic effort to convey a then new machine in an intelligible manner. This logical display of the bond between the artwork and the method, of computer graphics and program code, became a prerequisite of that which, in art and architecture, would eventually lead to a new faith in the mathematics of the machine.

As if it were possible to push the hidden structure of an artwork and the computer from the inside to the outside, one made use of a double demystification: that of the artistic creative process on the one hand, and on the other that of the logic of the machine. The fact that a part of the stir created by the computer graphics paradoxically lies in the machine's functional logic is all the more evident given that, from a design perspective, demystifying the machine also means demystifying the author. The technical basis cancels out the question of artistic creativity when it is evident that the author is not only a machine, but also a simple set of systems.

Nake's intention to display the simplicity of the program code in order to show how complex, but also how aesthetic, structures generated by code can be, made a mockery of the conservative discussion about the relationship between art, architecture, authorship, and technology. At the same time, however, any discussion involving code was no longer just a means to an end, aimed at calculating a largest amount of data in the shortest amount of time; it now formed the conceptual basis for an aesthetic avant-garde.[25] Max Bense, for whom epistemological access to the world could only be found in the semiotic,

24 See "computer-grafik," published in the series *edition rot,* text 19, ed. by Max Bense and Elisabeth Walther, Stuttgart, 1965.

25 See Georg Trogemann and Jochen Viehoff, *CodeArt – Eine elementare Einführung in die Programmierung als künstlerische Praktik,* Vienna, New York, 2005.

```
 1 'BEGIN' 'COMMENT' SCHOTTER.,
 2 'REAL' R, PIHALB, PI4T.,
 3 'INTEGER' I.,
 4 'PROCEDURE' QUAD.,
 5 'BEGIN'
 6 'REAL' P1, Q1, PSI., 'INTEGER' S.,
 7 JE1.=5*I/264., JA1.=-JE1.,
 8 JE2.=PI4T*(1+I/264).,
   JA2.=PI4T*(1-I/264).,
 9 P1.=P+5+J1., Q1.=Q+5+J1.,
   PSI.=J2.,
10 LEER(P1+R*COS(PSI),
   Q1+R*SIN(PSI)).,
11 'FOR' S.=1 'STEP' 1 'UNTIL' 4 'DO'
12 'BEGIN' PSI.=PSI+PIHALB.,
13 LINE(P1+R*COS(PSI),Q1+R*SIN(PSI))
14 'END'., I.=I+1
15 'END' QUAD.,
16 R.=5*1.4142.,
17 PIHALB.=3.14159*.5., PI4T.=PIHALB*.5.,
18 I.=0.,
19 SERIE(10.0,10.0,22,12,QUAD)
20 'END' SCHOTTER.,
```

Fig. 4: Georg Nees' Graphic *Schotter* (left) and the computer code, that generated the graphic, 1968. From: Georg Nees, *Generative Computergraphik*, 1969.

saw Nake's and Nees' programmed graphic as the first eyewitnesses to a future technical world of which he had always spoken so passionately. Bense wrote in his essay on "Projekte generativer Ästhetik" (Generative aesthetics projects), published in 1965 in his fundamental book *Aesthetica:* "In general [...] the 'artificial' differs from the 'natural' production category by the introduction of a *Vermittlungsschema* (communication schema) between the creator and the work that consists of a program and a program language, which introduces an unusual division of labor to the aesthetic process."[26] Bense was convinced that humans needed to be fully integrated into the world of science and technology, to intellectually incorporate themselves and to be incorporated by it.[27]

A Symbolic Machine as a Knowledge-Producing Object for Architecture?
The treatment of Bense's *Vermittlungsschema* marked an important difference between European and American origins of computer graphics. While the American version is mainly a history of tools without a philosophical foundation, in other words a history of pure tool building, the European, and in particular German, history of computer graphics often runs the risk of getting tangled up in an impenetrable web of philosophy and semiotics. The theory that is missing on one side is overabundant on the other. The lightness of one is the weight of the other.

Since "buildings without drawings"[28] and "programming culture in the design arts"[29] are popular topics today, it might be interesting to examine which of these two forms has actually proven more effective, useful, or to put it bluntly, better in one way or another for architecture. Nake shows us one productive way out of this comparison in his 1974 book entitled *Ästhetik als Informationsverarbeitung* (Aesthetics as Information Processing).[30] There is a short section in the book where he speculates about the computer's potential influence on architecture. Nake makes an assumption that would interest any

26 Max Bense, *Aesthetica. Einführung in die neue Aesthetik,* Baden-Baden, 1965, p. 338.
27 See Max Bense, *Technische Existenz. Essays,* Stuttgart, 1949.
28 See Mike Silver (ed.), *Programming Cultures* (Special Issue), *Architectural Design* 76 (July 2006), pp. 46–56.
29 Silver, ibid., pp. 5–11.
30 Frieder Nake, *Ästhetik als Informationsverarbeitung. Grundlagen der Informatik im Bereich ästhetischer Produktion und Kritik,* Vienna, New York, 1974.

architect designing with a computer today, who contextualizes his or her actions, or, who constantly questions how the computer changes his or her ideas regarding architecture. He states that architects had an experience similar to that of linguists "when trying to solve problems with computers [...]. They discovered that their knowledge about their field of expertise was greatly limited. The infiltration of a new machine, a new production instrument, proved to be an inspirer and a motivator. It was a source of new insight, and an innovative means of gaining knowledge."[31]

These are two interesting sentences. Nake presents us with a bouquet of metaphors in an attempt to illustrate both the computer's function and relevance for architects. He also refers to linguistics, which is presumably a reference to the revolutionary wave of inspiration at end of the 1950s brought on by the work of computer linguist Noam Chomsky,[32] which caught the attention of not only Bense, but also of architects such as Christopher Alexander. Nake goes on to speak of the "infiltration of a new machine" into architecture, of "production instruments," of "inspirer and a motivator," and of the "source." Not only for "new knowledge," but – and Nake now makes a fine differentiation – also for a "means of gaining knowledge." At first this use of metaphors might seem random, and perhaps even a bit excessive. But that is not the case at all. Nake is trying to describe something that is very difficult to visualize for the field of architecture and computer. He is producing conceptual images of research.

Nake's term "production instrument" is based on an interesting premise. He claims that the computer led architects to discover that "their knowledge about their field of expertise was greatly limited."[33] Could this be a symbolic machine as a knowledge-producing object for architecture? Is it merely a challenging assumption or perhaps the sharp observation of a mathematician, who students, in the 1960s in Stuttgart, wanted as a professor of architecture?[34] What is actually produced in architecture by, and with, the computer? And what role does this so-called production instrument actually play for the process of

31 Nake, ibid., p. 332.

32 See Noam Chomsky, *Syntactic Structures,* The Hague, Paris, 1957.

33 Nake, see note 30, p. 332.

34 Frieder Nake, letter to the author, April 28, 2008.

research to which Nake refers metaphorically in his statement? It seems architecture finds itself in a paradox, one that Gropius with his question may well have anticipated, but whose detailed contours he could never have imagined. Operating with code contradicts the inherent wealth of gesture in drawing, in its function as a principal cultural medium. However, this absence of gesture, or the "language without gesture," enables a multifarious and perhaps provocative view of architecture. Because Nake attempts to describe this metaphorically, he does not actually formulate an answer to Gropius's original question. He rather shifts the line of vision: architecture does not look to code, code looks to architecture.

The seemingly contradictory, unresearched field of drawing, programming, and gesture (understood as a concealing and revealing of code) might be an instructive point of departure for a new narrative of architectural history, that is, not traditionally as an account of construction and style, but as an account of technical systems and practices. It might also lead to understanding the shift of focus from the "product of meaning" to the "production of meaning"[35] in today's media and cultural sciences, not only as an incidental and secondary means of interpretation, but as a means of interpretation with a fundamentally different emphasis and that is accepted as thoroughly equivalent. The code's middle-man, which Bense called the *Vermittlungsschema,* can be developed into an architectural and media historical interpretation of architecture, via a critical comparison of both practices – of the natural and the artificial, of drawing and programming.

35 "Editorial," in *Zeitschrift für Medien- und Kulturforschung,* ed. by Lorenz Engell and Bernhard Siegert, Hamburg, 2009.

Andrea Gleiniger

STYLE OR CODE – ON THE PARADIGMS OF ARCHITECTURAL EXPRESSION TODAY

In which code do we *want* to build? This could be a new version of "In which style should we build?"[1] – the question raised by the architect Heinrich Hübsch almost 200 years ago. Formulated rhetorically as the title of a book, it contemporized the greatest concern of architecture during the first decade of the nineteenth century, and one which would continue to dominate the architectural discourse for the next 100 years: the search for an architectural expression that would correspond to the modern era of industrialization, commercialization, and globalization, as well as the new building challenges, innovative materials, and progress in construction technology brought forward by this era.

The adaptation of Hübsch's question implies that the concept of code is capable of replacing the concept of style – a possibility that postmodernism greatly encouraged. Charles Jencks, who extracted ever more codes out of the configurations and concepts of the current development of architecture and its inventions, operates precisely from this spirit.[2] We entrusted Jencks with such a question, even though he focuses less on the explorations of those posing the questions rather than on the self-confidence of those providing the programmatic answers. Because Jencks, in his tireless efforts to identify and proclaim new codes, very casually included into his various lines of argument the paradigm shift that had placed an information-technological code next to a more semiotic-related code. In doing so, he brought code, in terms of a technological concretion as an algorithmic basis for design, back into the discourse, and thus

1 Heinrich Hübsch, *In welchem Style sollen wir bauen?* (1828), Karlsruhe, 1984.

2 For Charles Jencks' representation and comments concerning the code concept, see the essay by Claus Dreyer entitled "Architectural Codes from a Semiotic Perspective" in this book, pp. 55–74. Meanwhile, semiotics, which originally so strongly influenced the concept of code, has also discovered the style discourse. With this in mind, the 11th International Congress of the German Association for Semiotic Studies (DGS) from June 24–26, 2005, at the European University Viadrina in Frankfurt/Oder, under the motto "In which Style Do We Want to Build?" was dedicated to the topic, *Stil als Zeichen, Funktionen – Brüche – Inszenierungen* (Style as Signs. Function – Interruptions – Orchestrations). The contributions to this conference have been published in the form of a CD (University publications – series of publications of the European University Viadrina, vol. 24, CD-ROM, ISSN 0941-7540, Frankfurt/Oder, 2006). It can also be accessed at http://www.sw2.euv-frankfurt-o.de/downloads/dgs11/index.htm.

helped it attain a new and, as might be predicted, also highly seminal significance for architecture and architectural design.

It is interesting to note that the postmodernist code theory no longer, or rarely, appears in context with the style discourse that has reemerged as an object of architectural theory.[3] This is somewhat surprising because, in the upswing of information theory, linguistics, and semiotics, the concept of code undoubtedly represented an attempt to do more than merely solve the dilemmas of a style theory that *sui generis* felt called upon to subject itself to self-examination. It also seemed appropriate, because it brought to light in a very contemporary manner that which the various, competing "postmodernist" architectural approaches attempted to address in a variety of ways: complexity and communication, or in other words: meaning. In light of the semiotic approach to the world's plural and complex qualities, code soon became an essential metaphor[4] – particularly in the context of architecture. At the same time, the initially linguistics-oriented code metaphor is not only a possibility of understanding complexities. It also seems to be the more suitable means of identifying social and cultural differences than the concept of style, which was beginning to wear. The social differentiation of code was complemented by a new legitimization of the various social spheres and publics as the aesthetic reference system. At the same time, and also comparable with Roland Barthes' perspective, the concept of code could be a means of critically assessing the old, redundant, idealistic ideas of a normative aesthetic judgment that is based on expertise and an elite sense of style.[5]

If we now attempt in the following to briefly analyze how these two concepts relate to the architectural context, it becomes clear that present findings have their previous history (or stories) in this conceptual examination, as in our

3 See note 2, and Ákos Moravánszky (ed.) in collaboration with Katalin M. Gyöngy, *Architekturtheorie im 20. Jahrhundert. Eine kritische Anthologie,* Vienna, 2003; and Achim Hahn, *Architekturtheorie. Wohnen, Entwerfen, Bauen,* Constance, 2008.

4 Eco defines semiotics as a discipline that "examines all cultural phenomena as processes of communication." This implies architecture as well, for which, through Eco, the term "code" was so explicitly applied. Translated from Umberto Eco, *Einführung in die Semiotik,* Munich, 1972.

5 See Roland Barthes, *The Semiotic Challenge* (1985), New York, 1988; and ibid., *Criticism and Truth* (1966), London, 1987.

previous discussions.[6] A previous history however, also concerning the concept of code, which places us in a state already described by the English and comparative literature specialist K. Ludwig Pfeiffer in relation to the discursive oscillation of the style theory: "Those (still) occupied with the style concept will soon find themselves in a strange state of uncertainty." And they will have to "contend with its diffuse omnipresence [...] and complain about the incomprehensibilities of its implications." This can also be compared with the concept of code. And when Pfeiffer adds that "[t]heoretically repeatedly proclaimed dead, haunted by permanent difficulties of definition, the style theory, in terms of practice, has remained as tough as ever,"[7] it can also be maintained that precisely this erratic history of meaning within different contexts is what keeps the concept of code vibrant.

Style's Claim to Validity as an Aesthetic and Social Agreement

"More was written about architecture in Germany between 1750 and 1800 than at any other moment in time. [...] The concepts at the heart of this vibrant discussion, in which not only architects participated, were order and distortion, taste and character in building and construction. [...] Special attention was paid, albeit several decades later than in the other arts, to the debate on taste that began at the onset of the century."[8] This debate, which took place during the transition from absolutism to bourgeois society, was centered on developing criteria and points of reference for a new social order. "Taste is not only the ideal created by a new society, but we see this 'good taste' producing what was subsequently called 'good society.' It no longer recognizes and legitimizes itself

6 See the previous volumes of the series *Context Architecture* entitled *Simulation, Complexity, and Pattern.*

7 Translated from Hans Ulrich Gumbrecht and K. Ludwig Pfeiffer (eds.) in collaboration with Armin Biermann, Thomas Müller, Bernd Schulte, and Barbara Ullrich, *Stil. Geschichte und Funktionen eines kulturwissenschaftlichen Diskurselements,* Frankfurt am Main, 1986, pp. 685–725, here: p. 685 and p. 693.

8 Translated from Klaus Jan Philipp, "'Von der Wirkung der Baukunst auf die Veredelung der Menschen.' Anmerkungen zur deutschen Architekturtheorie um 1800," in *Revolutionsarchitektur. Ein Aspekt der europäischen Architektur um 1800,* exhibition catalog Deutsches Architekturmuseum Frankfurt, ed. by Winfried Nerdinger, Klaus Jan Philipp, and Hans-Peter Schwarz, Munich, 1990, pp. 43–47, here: p. 47.

on the basis of birth and rank but simply through the shared nature of its judgments or, rather, its capacity to rise above narrow interests and private predilections to the title of judgment."[9] This concept of taste points to a higher understanding that is not only entirely unrelated to the concept of fashion, which was later introduced to the notion of taste. On the contrary, taste actually becomes the central category of an idealistic, normative aesthetic: in that it refers to the universal "under which it is to be subsumed." In "view of the whole," which subjects taste to specific terms, the concept of taste merges with the concept of style, and refers in turn to style's agreements.[10] The claim to validity related with style becomes the system of reference for aesthetic verdicts and decisions that are rooted in education and knowledge.

If it had been so important to establish taste and style as points of reference for setting norms and generating meaning, given the insecurities associated with the onset of industrialized modernism, then this was to a large extent due to the shift of weight from a courtly to a bourgeois society and the social and cultural phenomena related to this transition. Secondly, it entailed the fact that, in the course of industrialization, the emerging guild of engineers increasingly questioned the building capabilities of architects.

A major chance for the guild of architects to uphold its artistic authorship was by affirming the style decisions based on architecture's laboriously established artistic claims and by defending the interpretive sovereignty of "taste." Furthermore, architects even became the "aesthetic educators of the public." Their works were aimed at "refining the public through architecture."[11] In adapting the idealistic aesthetics of Friedrich Schiller, architects proposed a programmatic alternative version of the engineer, whose abilities were primarily aimed at serving innovative functionality.

It also concerned a type of "medial" publicity value of architecture as an instrument of aesthetic and ideological orientation. The special aspect of this intention was not to target the cultural and social elite, who traditionally had

9 Hans-Georg Gadamer, *Truth and Method,* translation ed. by Garrett Barden and John Cumming, New York, 1975, p. 32.

10 Ibid., p. 34: "[...] Both taste and power of judgment evaluate the object in relation to the whole in order to see whether it fits in with everything else – that is, whether it is 'fitting.'" And referring to the related note 67: "This is where the concept of style has its place."

11 See note 8, p. 44.

access to the possibilities of following and understanding aesthetic decisions in detail. It applied more to the growing masses, who, without detailed knowledge, were geared to the guidelines of the elite.

The actual significance and monumental consequence of the style decision was demonstrated by the legendary experimental arrangement presented by Karl Friedrich Schinkel in the 1820s in his divergent designs for the construction of the Friedrichswerder Church in Berlin.[12]

The different stylistic proposals were less representative of the split soul of an architect who based his designs on two different aesthetic paradigms – each proposal actually embodied a very different program.[13] According to the "style" that was chosen, particular codes would assemble, so to speak, that made distinct statements about the political, social, and artistic stances of the architectural design.

Ever since Heinrich Hübsch had gone public with his programmatic question, the discussion on style assumed a great role in the architectural discourse. And if this debate was, on the one hand, synonymous with the search for architecture's and art's fundamental definitions and these disciplines' stances on social and cultural issues, as for instance according to Gottfried Semper[14] or the art historian Alois Riegel, then the style question, on the other hand, also became increasingly politicized, at least in Germany. The decision of a particular style would lead to the manifestation of a certain *Weltanschauung* (world view).[15]

Even the increasingly urgent reformist responses, at the threshold of the twentieth century, to the disorientation and challenges triggered by the modern age were concerned with integrating reformist concepts into one,

12 "Classic" or "gothic" were the diverging stylistic premises of his designs for the church, built from 1824 onwards, which was to serve both the German and the French parishioners.

13 On the one hand, Schinkel's designs were characterized by an archeologically substantiated reference to antiquity and its architectural reception in buildings constructed during the Italian renaissance as a basis for a new classicism. On the other hand, the designs reflected the increased significance of the Middle Ages which, in the form of gothic style, were viewed as an ideal and desired image of a present preoccupied with the search for a new and unique national identity.

14 See Gottfried Semper's incomplete opus magnum, *Der Stil in den technischen und tektonischen Künsten, oder Praktische Aesthetik. Ein Handbuch für Techniker, Künstler und Kunstfreunde,* Frankfurt am Main, 1860–1863.

15 See also Hanno-Walter Kruft, *Geschichte der Architekturtheorie. Von der Antike bis zur Gegenwart,* Munich, 1985, p. 359ff.

comprehensive cultural aspiration, and transferring them into new aesthetic and cultural commitments.[16]

At the same time, however, the view of the style phenomenon became differentiated in a way that would determine the future understanding of the style theory. In addition to the "styles of thought," to which the field of philosophy laid special claim, it was the modern, social sciences and the upcoming discipline of cultural sociology in particular that, in light of the social dynamic of the modern urbanization processes, diagnosed specific "life styles,"[17] and thus ultimately directed the gaze to the enigmatic phenomenon of "fashion" and – without it being named as such – the associated "codes." Umberto Eco, to whom we are indebted decades later for developing the concept of code in the 1970s to become a core premise in architectural theory, arrives at a crucial conclusion when he speaks of "styling" as being a characteristic of the code: "The spinning spiral in which our times fill forms with signifiers and in turn empty them out, rediscovers codes and never forgets them again, and is basically nothing more than a never-ending styling operation."[18]

The paradox lay in the fact that style on the one hand was questioned again and again as a "metaprogram," yet the longing for the one, unified epoch style that would re-establish the lost coherence had (still) not expired. Thus, "behind the rejection of styles,"[19] which so programmatically pervades modernism, there is also the determination to establish a style in the sense of a comprehensive concept that "believes [however] that the only correct 'moral' position of the architect lies in a systematic pursuit, directed at essential, justi-

16 For instance in the case of Otto Wagner, Hermann Muthesius, Adolf Loos, or Hendrik Petrus Berlage. For an overview and summary of the most important positions regarding the issue of style, see Ákos Moravánszky, "Vom Stilus zum Branding," see note 3, pp. 7–120.

17 See here Georg Simmel, "Der Bilderrahmen. Ein ästhetischer Versuch" (1902), in *Aufsätze und Abhandlungen 1901–1908, Band I, Georg Simmel: Gesamtausgabe,* ed. by Otthein Rammstedt, vol. 7, ed. by Rüdiger Kramme, Angela Rammstedt, and Otthein Rammstedt, Frankfurt am Main, 1995, pp. 101–108, here: p. 105; or Georg Simmel, "Das Problem des Stils" (1908), in *Aufsätze und Abhandlungen 1901–1908, Band II, Georg Simmel: Gesamtausgabe,* ed. by Otthein Rammstedt, vol. 8, ed. by Alessandro Cavalli and Volkhard Krech, Frankfurt am Main, 1993, pp. 374–384, here: p. 382.

18 Translated from Umberto Eco, *Einführung in die Semiotik,* Munich, 1972, p. 314, here: p. 321.

19 Translated from Werner Oechslin, *Stilhülse und Kern. Otto Wagner, Adolf Loos und der evolutionäre Weg der modernen Architektur,* Zurich, Berlin, 1994, p. 37.

fied contexts and principles,"[20] and hence not in merely postulating a type of idealistic claim to education. It was also meant to ensure the (re)unification of the disparate and estranged fields of art, technology, and life.

The selection made by Henry-Russel Hitchcock and Philip Johnson,[21] presented in 1932 in an exhibition under the title "International Style" and which unfurled its sustained effect in a book, was not met with complete agreement by the architects of the time, who were positioning themselves in various ways within the (classic) modernist movement. Yet this does not change the fact that the different avant-garde concepts all lined up under this one designing standard, which permeated all areas of life aesthetically and conceptually. Within this still emphatically voiced aesthetic and conceptual designing standard, in which "practical culture" and "aesthetic" culture were to unite, a conception of style emerged that was yet again "idealistic" in nature: "The program represented by the avant-garde, comprised of the much-quoted dissolution of art in the practice of life, still contains at its core the idealistic position that supports a possible unity of the differentiated and estranged parts of life: that functionally designed architecture would become practical culture, in which the theoretical aspects of culture are already incorporated and further promoted."[22]

From "International Style" to "Good Form"

This "idealistic" gesture did not only endure until the 1950s and 1960s, in Germany it also gains new meaning in light of the experience of the Third Reich: a

20 Ibid.

21 Johnson, who over the course of his life advanced from a young propagandist of modernism to the figurehead of an at times equally bold and simplistic postmodernism, is yet aware of the sensitive issues involved in the concept of style, especially in light of his own biography, e.g. when he stated in 1988 in connection with his exhibition, *Deconstructive Architecture*: "It is now about sixty years since Henry-Russell Hitchcock, Alfred Barr and I started our quest for a new style of architecture which would, like Gothic or Romanesque in their day, take over the discipline of our art. The resulting exhibition of 1932, 'Modern Architecture,' summed up the architecture of the twenties [...] and prophesied an International Style in architecture to take the place of the 'romantic' styles of the previous half century. With this exhibition, there are no such aims." Philip Johnson and Mark Wigley, *Deconstructive Architecture,* exhibition catalog Museum of Modern Art New York, New York, London, 1988.

22 Translated from Michael Müller, "Die Versöhnung der 'theoretischen Kultur' mit der 'praktischen Kultur' – eine Vision der Moderne," in *Vision der Moderne. Das Prinzip Konstruktion,* ed. by Heinrich Klotz in collaboration with Volker Fischer, Andrea Gleiniger, and Hans-Peter Schwarz, Munich, 1986, pp. 33–45, here: p. 34.

unified formal language originating from standardization and abstraction leads to the generation of a new pathos of taste and morality: "good form"![23]

It is only a small step from the potential claim to absoluteness of a "good form," which invokes the "morality of objects,"[24] to the idea of "programming the beautiful." Moreover, it is not surprising that this step was made within the walls of, or even in the intellectual catchment area of, the very educational institution that after the Second World War had nurtured the contemporary adaptation of the Bauhaus legacy in a very specific manner: the Ulm School of Design, headed by Max Bill, an uncompromising aesthetic educator, and Max Bense, a philosopher with magisterial ambition. Bense's intent was a synthesis of aesthetics and technology, in order to complete the move from the normative modernist aesthetic of "programming taste" to that of "programming the beautiful" from the spirit of information theory.[25]

Bense and his artistically ambitious comrades-in-arms, such as the mathematicians Frieder Nake and Georg Nees, dreamed of the aesthetic energy of the code as a basis of programming the beautiful, but they were not explicitly hoping that a new style would emerge from the alliance between aesthetics and code. They were actually aiming for the opposite: namely for an aesthetics that was liberated from every ideological implication, and that would be further "objectified" in the technological production process. At the same time, however, a type of certainty resulted from this objectification, which would put a definite end to all style discussions and thus finally establish a new moral claim to validity – a claim that was aimed less at the plural coexistence of an (infinite) number of possibilities, the very option that today describes the true fascination of the code. The intention was more to optimize the complexity in the

23 The term "good form" became the epitome of modern functional design in the 1950s after the 1949 exhibition in the Zürcher Kunstgewerbemuseum (Zurich Museum of Arts and Crafts) and the resulting publication by Max Bill, *Die gute Form. Wanderausstellung des Schweizerischen Werkbundes,* Zurich, 1949; as well as: *Die gute Form. 6 Jahre Auszeichnung "Die gute Form" an der Schweizer Mustermesse in Basel,* ed. by the management of the Swiss Federal Samples Fair in Basel [et al.], Winterthur, 1957.

24 The title of the 1987 exhibition on the history and aftereffects of the Hochschule für Gestaltung Ulm (Ulm School of Design). See Herbert Lindinger (ed.), *Hochschule für Gestaltung Ulm. Die Moral der Gegenstände,* exhibition catalog Hfg-Archiv Ulm, Berlin, 1987.

25 Georg Vrachliotis, *Geregelte Verhältnisse. Architektur und technisches Denken in der Epoche der Kybernetik,* Vienna, New York (forthcoming in 2010).

abstraction, from which ultimately a new aesthetic-stylistic apodictic would have developed (and in parts did develop) as a type of cultural side effect.

In this regard, Bense and his comrades-in-arms joined the many-voiced choir of protests and the architectural break-away movements that aimed to distance themselves from the simplification strategies and the equally "restrictive" as redundant (still influenced by the guiding principles of the industrial age) architectural "code" of postwar modernism. For instance when, via the paradigm of structure, attention was shifted to a new basic research that was both constructively functional as well as cultural. This is similar to a certain kind of structuralist research, theoretically represented above all by Christian Norberg-Schulz, or soon after the archetypical research of Italian rationalism, in particular as continued in altered form by Aldo Rossi. The concepts of "structure" and of "archetype" have in this case some similarities with the concept of code, which is applied in the sense of a comprehensive and essential artistic statement.

If the aesthetically ambitious concept of code of information technology aimed to optimize the handling of complexity, the linguistic and semiotic code concept, which had been introduced to the discussion almost simultaneously, had in certain respects the opposite intentions. The aesthetically ambitious concept of code was oriented toward diversification and differentiation, which was to take account of social, societal, and cultural complexity and plurality. Against this backdrop, code gained new relevance also for architecture. Thus, all architects who were searching for architectural contexts of meaning that transcended purely functional and economic rationalism rediscovered the relationship between code and complexity under the banner of communications and sign theories.

The crisis of functionalist architecture and the accompanying loss of meaning caused a whole range of disciplines to spring into action, which meant that the problem of architecture became interdisciplinary in ways in which this had never been the case before, or at least not in this socially oriented manner. Disciplines such as sociology, psychology, semiotics, and communications theory were now entering the ring of architectural discourse, so as to find or invent systems of reference for architecture that would contribute to generating and legitimizing architectural meaning in other than the traditional aesthetic manner.

Fig. 1: Robert Venturi and John Rauch: *Guild House,* Philadelphia, 1960–1963. An example of different social codes clashing: a temporary golden television antenna, removed at the time of the photograph, and the arched thermal windows.

In this fashion, Werner Durth, in his 1977 examination of the state of contemporary urban design, appropriates not only Umberto Eco's but also Manfred Kiemle's attempt to solve the "aesthetic problems of architecture" by means of information theory.[26] Durth examines the city and architecture from a socio-semiotic perspective, and makes the role of the code a basic element of his diagnosis of the "staging of the everyday world": "Along the path of the individual 'search for identity,' i.e. among the unfathomable number of different value systems, life forms, and situational structures, any indication that allows the identification of fields of experience and action is important. In the process, visual codes and cognitive competences, shaped by a colloquially conveyed everyday experience, form the filter through which the perceptions and impressions of urban environments are processed subjectively, and through which corresponding images are shaped and situations defined."[27]

However, even before Eco's *Semiotics* helped open new perspectives on the semantic dimensions of architecture, Robert Venturi had already set the tone in the mid-60s with his unbiased and intelligent plea for complexity, which was argued from the depth of architectural history by means of past and present codes [Fig. 1]. Through Denise Scott Brown this plea gained a sociological and urbanistic dimension.

The experiment of such a "revision of modernism" that was based on a plural system of reference, occurs – as we know – in the conflicting field of extremes: between "E and U architecture," between high-tech and *arte povera,* between Las Vegas and Levittown,[28] between Gian Lorenzo Bernini and Le

26 Regarding Eco, see note 4. In fact, Eco did not waste any thoughts on theoretical differentiation and casually equated code with style of art or manners: "In the last century, one could have been witness to a typical phenomenon of art history, namely that in a given time a code (a style of art, a manner) implied an ideology [...]." Translated from Umberto Eco, *Einführung in die Semiotik,* Munich, 1972, p. 314. See also Manfred Kiemle, *Ästhetische Probleme der Architektur unter dem Aspekt der Informationsästhetik,* Quickborn, 1967.

27 Translated from Werner Durth, *Inszenierung der Alltagswelt. Zur Kritik der Stadtgestaltung* (series *Bauwelt Fundamente*), Braunschweig, 1977, p. 177.

28 The sociologist Herbert J. Gans, who taught at the University of Pennsylvania in Philadelphia, played a significant role for Denise Scott Brown and Robert Venturi, not least because of his view of the sociological constellation of the American suburb, as examined through the example of Levittown/Pennsylvania. Through Gans, Brown and Venturi became interested not only in the suburb but also in the phenomenon of Main Street, which they studied on the example of the Las Vegas Strip (1972). See also: Herbert J. Gans, *The Levittowners: Ways of Life and Politics in a New Suburban Community,* New York, 1967.

Corbusier. If nothing else, architects continued to search in this field of conflict for their disciplinary self-will and for new (architectural) artistic self-assertion.

However, whether it involves a new concept of style(s) or the notion of code which primes the search for the different ways of interpreting architecture and the architectural or urban planning context, this is at first unimportant for the increasingly acute discourse of postmodernism. It is far more crucial that it concerns – in one way or another – meaning that transcends the purely functional.

Yet, this is not only a matter of the trite play of words that can be derived from Louis Sullivan's motto "form follows function," and which makes "fiction" of "function." Particularly in the European postmodern context, it also concerns a recovery (and salvage of honor) of architecture as art and not only as social, functional, and constructive technology.

"Schöner Schein"[29] Versus "Information"

This becomes even clearer when viewed from the perspective outlined by Heinrich Klotz in the catalog introduction for the opening exhibition of the Deutsches Architekturmuseum in Frankfurt am Main in 1984. In light of the buildings and projects by Charles Moore and Robert Venturi, and by Aldo Rossi and O. M. Ungers, he noted that, "[f]or all their differences, the architects mentioned here, Moore, Venturi, Rossi, and Ungers, share a common goal. Not only do they want to present symbolic and typological forms in the foreground purely as a way of communicating content, they also want to use them as the material of fiction, allowing a building to become a work of art once again, a 'fair illusion.'"[30]

29 Different to the following English translation of Heinrich Klotz's quote, the translation of *Schöner Schein* should be "beautiful appearance," or possibly "the appearance of beauty." I am following a suggestion made by Mark Kyburz, whose research in this matter is greatly appreciated.

30 "The building should be a mode of portrayal, not merely a functional tool. [...] The various tendencies of postmodernist architecture come together in their striving to see a building as a creation of 'fair illusion.'" Heinrich Klotz in the introduction to *Postmodern Visions. Drawings, Paintings, and Models by Contemporary Architects,* ed. by Heinrich Klotz, with essays by Volker Fischer, Andrea Gleiniger, Heinrich Klotz, and Hans-Peter Schwarz, New York, 1985, p. 10.

In this context, the surprising aspect of Klotz's plea in favor of postmodern was not the concept of fiction he used here – as in other areas – to argue against the concept of function and for new horizons of meaning in architecture. What was surprising, however, is that he seized the concept of "information" and set it against the idealistic *topos* of *Schöner Schein* – because, this comparison actually contained a plea in favor of style and against code,[31] or, at least indirectly. The declaration in favor of this *Schöner Schein* led, in context of postmodernism, to many misunderstandings. However, when making his plea, Klotz most certainly did not refer to the superficial facade cosmetics through which the conceptual origins of "postmodernism" so quickly compromised themselves. He was more likely interested in the *Karnevalskerzendunst,* or the "haze of the carnival candle," which Gottfried Semper once declared the true atmosphere of art.[32]

To perceive of the work of architectural art as a work of *Schöner Schein* implied the claim that an idea has condensed to become an aesthetic form or, formulated conversely, an aesthetic form is not possible without an idea. A notion such as this breathes life back into the idealistic concept of style.

The questions as to whether postmodernism generated a new style or a new code, or whether it is in itself a new style or merely an ominous framework for both an ambitious and arbitrary "styling" (Eco), have yet to be discussed thoroughly – which might not be all that essential. New impulses may however develop in terms of changing the concept of code.

Different to its metaphoric appropriations in regards to a postmodern architectural system of language, the concept of code has now become an operative key concept of design. Reformulating the concept of code in the terms of information technology has given new energy to it.

31 We have reason to assume that Heinrich Klotz deliberately positioned himself against Charles Jencks.

32 See here among others, Moravánszky, 2003, see note 3, p. 9.

Fig. 2: Peter Eisenman: Institute for Biochemistry, project for the "Rebstockgelände," Frankfurt, 1987.

From Metaphor to Operation

In this development, a pivotal role needs to be accorded to the work of Peter Eisenman. As early as 1987 the American architect and one of the original "New York Five"[33] adapted the notion of code as a biological metaphor for an architectural concept in his design for the Institute of Biochemistry in Frankfurt [Fig. 2]. Moreover, Eisenman has also continued to consolidate the various aspects of meaning that underlie the notions of coding (and codification). His project for Santiago de Compostela is a case in point, for here on the one hand he refers to the religious traditions of the *codici* in terms of a system of rules that generates a world view, and on the other hand he operates and experiments with an instrumentarium of information technology as a means of design strategy.[34]

Fiction Versus Narration

Postmodernism programmatically linked "code" to the function of story telling, meaning theories of fictionalization in which histories and narratives could be designed architecturally as contextualizing references, and then put very consciously into practice. Compared with the more static concept of fiction, the concept of "narration" reveals the processual aspects behind the act of narration that materializes architecturally less through images than via influences.

If one speaks today of "story telling with code," then it concerns a new quality of architectural narration[35] that is produced not (only) from a semantic and metaphorical understanding of code, but rather from its operational and operative scope of possibilities. The code becomes a source and focus of a complex architectural experiment that can be influenced in a variety of ways by nature, environment, technology, culture, and history – for instance in the 2009

33 The name comes from an exhibition entitled *Five Architects,* in which Eisenman, Michael Graves, Charles Gwathmey, John Hejduk, and Richard Meier asserted their criticism of architecture of the 1960s in connection with a programmatic reference to Le Corbusier. A corresponding book was published in 1975: *Five Architects: Eisenman, Graves, Gwathmey, Hejduk, Meier,* New York, 1975.

34 See Cynthia Davidson (ed.), *Code X. The City of Culture of Galicia,* New York, 2005; Luca Galofaro (ed.), *Digital Eisenman. An Office of the Electronic Era,* Basel, Boston, Berlin, 1999.

35 See the essay by Gabriele Gramelsberger, "Story Telling with Code" in this volume, pp. 29–40.

Fig. 3: New Monte Rosa mountain hut with the Matterhorn at the back, view from the southeast.

project involving the Monte Rosa mountain hut in Zermatt [Fig. 3], where the design was inspired by a highly complex layering of functional and contextual conditions[36] and oscillates between tent and metal hut, crystal and stone block.

If the need exists to not (only) sort today's architectural concepts according to a mainly semantically based concept of code, but rather gain new definitional energy from the scope of possibilities of the operational code – which might also inject new meaning into a culturally contaminated theory such as style – style could once again mean recognizing that "the position of the architect lies in a systematic pursuit, directed at essential, justified contexts and principles."[37] In light of the fact that many architects see the concept of code as a threat to their creative authorship an unbiased use of code theory in architecture is a challenge. Taking it on would mean understanding consciousness of style not as "branding," but rather as a particular position, as an artistic and cultural trace that indicates an architectural interrelation between work and life.

36 The new Monte Rosa mountain hut is a collaborative project of ETH Zurich, SAC – Swiss Alpine Club, Lucerne University of Applied Sciences and Arts – Technology & Architecture, and Empa – Swiss Federal Laboratories for Materials Testing and Research. The many factors that influenced the design of this exposed site include the ecosystem and energy self-sufficiency, the climatic conditions, the internal and external functional requirements, the production conditions of the hut and its material technology, as well as numerous other factors. See also http://www.neuemonterosa-huette.ch.
37 See note 19.

SELECTED LITERATURE

This selected bibliography lists the texts referred to by the authors of this volume, supplemented with additional texts of relevance. Entries are listed chronologically. Where feasible and useful, dates of first or original editions have been cited.

—

Heinrich Hübsch, *In welchem Style sollen wir bauen?* (1828), Karlsruhe, 1984.

—

Gottfried Semper, *Der Stil in den technischen und tektonischen Künsten, oder Praktische Aesthetik. Ein Handbuch für Techniker, Künstler und Kunstfreunde,* Frankfurt am Main, 1860–1863.

—

Georg Simmel, "Der Bilderrahmen. Ein ästhetischer Versuch" (1902), in *Aufsätze und Abhandlungen 1901–1908, Band I, Georg Simmel: Gesamtausgabe,* ed. by Otthein Rammstedt, vol. 7, ed. by Rüdiger Kramme, Angela Rammstedt and Otthein Rammstedt, Frankfurt am Main, 1995, pp. 101–108.

—

Ernst Cassirer, *Substance and Function, and Einstein's Theory of Reality* (1910), Chicago, London, 1923.

—

Claude E. Shannon, "The Mathematical Theory of Communication," in *Bell System Technical Journal* 27 (July and October 1948), pp. 379–423 and pp. 623–656.

—

Norbert Wiener, *Cybernetics. Or Communication and Control in the Animal and the Machine,* Cambridge/Mass., 1948.

—

Erwin Schrödinger, *What Is Life? The Physical Aspect of the Living Cell,* Cambridge/UK, 1944.

—

Max Bense, *Technische Existenz. Essays,* Stuttgart, 1949.

—

Noam Chomsky, *Syntactic Structures,* The Hague, Paris, 1957.

—

Hans-Georg Gadamer, *Truth and Method* (1960), New York, 1975.

—

Ivan E. Sutherland, *Sketchpad. A Man-Machine Graphical Communication System,* Lincoln Laboratory Technical Report no. 296, Massachusetts Institute of Technology, January 1963.

—

John Backus, W. P. Heising, "FORTRAN," in *IEEE Trans. Electron. Comp.* 13, 1964, pp. 382–385.

—

"computer-grafik," published in the series *edition rot,* text 19, ed. by Max Bense and Elisabeth Walther, Stuttgart, 1965.

—

John von Neumann, *Theory of Self-Reproducing Automata,* Urbana, 1966, ed. and completed by Arthur W. Burks.

—

Roland Barthes, *Criticism and Truth* (1966), London, 1987.

—

Manfred Kiemle, *Ästhetische Probleme der Architektur unter dem Aspekt der Informationsästhetik,* Quickborn, 1967.

—

Marshall Nirenberg, *The Genetic Code. Nobel Lecture,* 1968, online: www.nobelprize.org.

—

Charles Jencks, George Baird (eds.), *Meaning in Architecture,* London, 1969.

—

David Evans, "Augmented Human Intellect," in *Computer Graphics in Architecture and Design. Proceedings of the Yale Conference on Architecture and Computer Graphics* (April 1968), ed. by Murray Milne, New Haven/Connecticut, 1969, p. 62ff.

—

Steve A. Coons, "Computer Aided Design," in *Computer Graphics in Architecture and Design. Proceedings of the Yale Conference on Architecture and Computer Graphics* (April 1968), ed. by Murray Milne, New Haven/Connecticut, 1969, p. 9ff.

—

Nicholas Negroponte, *The Architecture Machine Group,* Cambridge/Mass., 1970.

—

Gillo Dorfles, "Ikonologie und Semiotik in der Architektur," in *Architektur als Zeichensystem,* ed. by Alessandro Carline, Bernhard Schneider, Tübingen, 1971, pp. 91–98.

—

Umberto Eco, *Einführung in die Semiotik,* Munich, 1972.

—

Frieder Nake, *Ästhetik als Informationsverarbeitung. Grundlagen der Informatik im Bereich ästhetischer Produktion und Kritik,* Vienna, New York, 1974.

—

Werner Durth, *Inszenierung der Alltagswelt. Zur Kritik der Stadtgestaltung* (series *Bauwelt Fundamente*), Braunschweig, 1977.

—

Charles Jencks, *The Language of Post-Modern Architecture,* London, 1977.

—

Charles Jencks, "Post-Modern History," in *Architectural Design* 1 (1978).

—

John Backus, "Programming in America in the 1950s," in *A History of Computing in the Twentieth Century,* ed. by Nicholas Metropolis, J. Howlett, Gian-Carlo Rota, New York, 1980, pp. 125–135.

—

Geoffrey Broadbent, Richard Bunt, Charles Jencks (eds.), *Signs, Symbols, and Architecture,* Chichester, 1980.

—

Paul E. Ceruzzi, *A History of Modern Computing,* Cambridge/Mass., 1998.

—

Donald E. Knuth, Luis Trabb Pardo, "The Early Development of Programming Languages," in *A History of Computing in the Twentieth Century,* ed. by Nicholas Metropolis, J. Howlett, Gian-Carlo Rota, New York, 1980, pp. 197–273.

—

Werner Oechslin, "Geometrie und Linie. Die Vitruvianische 'Wissenschaft' von der Architekturzeichnung," in *Daidalos* 1 (1981), p. 20ff.

—

Heinrich Klotz, *The History of Postmodern Architecture* (1984), Cambridge/Mass., 1988.

—

Hanno-Walter Kruft, *Geschichte der Architekturtheorie. Von der Antike bis zur Gegenwart,* Munich, 1985.

—

Jürgen Habermas, "Modern and Postmodern Architecture" (1985), in J. Habermas, *The New Conservatism. Cultural Criticism and the Historian's Debate,* Cambridge/Mass., 1989.

—

Roland Barthes, *The Semiotic Challenge* (1985), New York, 1988.

—

Charles Jencks, *Towards a Symbolic Architecture. The Thematic House,* New York, 1985.

—

Heinrich Klotz (ed.), *Postmodern Visions. Drawings, Paintings, and Models by Contemporary Architects,* with essays by Volker Fischer, Andrea Gleiniger, Heinrich Klotz, and Hans-Peter Schwarz, New York, 1985.

—

Andreas Huyssen, Klaus Scherpe (eds.), *Postmoderne. Zeichen eines kulturellen Wandels,* Reinbek, 1986.

—

Hans Ulrich Gumbrecht, K. Ludwig Pfeiffer (eds.) in collaboration with Armin Biermann, Thomas Müller, Bernd Schulte, Barbara Ullrich, *Stil. Geschichte und Funktionen eines kulturwissenschaftlichen Diskurselements,* Frankfurt am Main, 1986.

—

Wolfgang Welsch, *Unsere postmoderne Moderne,* Weinheim, 1987.

—

Sybille Krämer, *Symbolische Maschinen*, Darmstadt, 1988.

—

Klaus Jan Philipp, "'Von der Wirkung der Baukunst auf die Veredelung der Menschen.' Anmerkungen zur deutschen Architekturtheorie um 1800," in *Revolutionsarchitektur. Ein Aspekt der europäischen Architektur um 1800,* exhibition catalog Deutsches Architekturmuseum Frankfurt, ed. by Winfried Nerdinger, Klaus Jan Philipp, Hans-Peter Schwarz, Munich, 1990, pp. 43–47.

—

Claus Dreyer, "Zitat und Zitieren in zeitgenössischer Architektur," in *Zeitschrift für Semiotik,* 14/1-2 (1992), pp. 41–59.

—

Werner Oechslin, *Stilhülse und Kern. Otto Wagner, Adolf Loos und der evolutionäre Weg der modernen Architektur,* Zurich, Berlin, 1994.

—

Claus Dreyer et al. (eds.), *Lebenswelt – Zeichenwelt. Life World – Sign World. Festschrift für Martin Krampen,* Lüneburg, 1994.

—

Norbert Bolz, Friedrich A. Kittler, Christoph Tholen (eds.), *Computer als Medium,* Munich, 1994.

—

Roland Posner, Klaus Robering, Thomas A. Sebeok (eds.), *Semiotik. Ein Handbuch zu den zeichentheoretischen Grundlagen von Natur und Kultur/Semiotics. A Handbook on the Sign-Theoretic Foundations of Nature and Culture,* vol. 1, Berlin, New York, 1997.

—

Eduard Führ, Hans Friesen, Anette Sommer (eds.), *Architektur – Sprache. Buchstäblichkeit, Versprachlichung, Interpretation,* Münster, 1998.

—

Hans Blumenberg, *Paradigms for a Metaphorology,* Ithaca (forthcoming in 2010).

—

Walter Koschatzky, *Die Kunst der Zeichnung. Technik, Geschichte, Meisterwerke,* Munich, 1999.

—

Luca Galofaro (ed.), *Digital Eisenman. An Office of the Electronic Era,* Basel, Boston, Berlin, 1999.

—

Winfried Nöth, *Handbuch der Semiotik,* 2nd. ed., Stuttgart, 2000.

—

Lily E. Kay, *Who Wrote the Book of Life. A History of the Genetic Code,* Stanford, 2000.

—

Ákos Moravánszky, "Vom Stilus zum Branding," in *Architekturtheorie des 20. Jahrhunderts,* ed. by Á. Moravánszky, Vienna, New York, 2003, pp. 7–120.

—

Hans Dieter Hellige, "Zur Genese des informatischen Programmbegriffs: Begriffbildung, metaphorische Prozesse, Leitbilder und professionelle Kulturen," in *Algorithmik, Kunst, Semiotik. Hommage für Frieder Nake,* ed. by Karl-Heinz Rödinger, Heidelberg, 2003, pp. 42–75.

—

Ingeborg Flagge, Romana Schneider (eds.), *Die Revision der Postmoderne,* exhibition catalog Deutsches Architekturmuseum Frankfurt, Hamburg, 2004.

—

Elijah Huge (ed.), *Perspecta 35: Building Codes, Yale architectural journal,* Cambridge/Mass., 2004.

—

Cynthia Davidson (ed.), *Code X. The City of Culture of Galicia,* New York, 2005.

—

Georg Trogemann, Jochen Viehoff, *CodeArt – Eine elementare Einführung in die Programmierung als künstlerische Praktik,* Vienna, New York, 2005.

—

Ingeborg M. Rocker, "When Code Matters," in *Architectural Design* 76/421 (2006), pp. 16–25.

—

Mike Silver (ed.), *Programming Cultures* (Special Issue), *Architectural Design* 76 (July 2006), pp. 46–56.

—

Eva Jablonka, Marion J. Lamb, *Evolution in Four Dimensions. Genetic, Epigenetic, Behavioral, and Symbolic Variation in the History of Life,* Cambridge/Mass., 2006.

—

Achim Hahn, *Architekturtheorie. Wohnen, Entwerfen, Bauen,* Constance, 2008.

—

Michael Silver, "Matter/in-formation," in Evan Douglis, *Autogenic Structures,* New York, 2009, pp. 152–191.

—

Claus Dreyer, "Semiotik und Ästhetik in der Architekturtheorie der sechziger Jahre," in *Kulturtechnik Entwerfen. Praktiken, Konzepte und Medien in Architektur und Design Science,* ed. by Daniel Gethmann and Susanne Hauser, Bielefeld, 2009, pp. 179–201.

—

Zeitschrift für Medien- und Kulturforschung, ed. by Lorenz Engell and Bernhard Siegert, Hamburg (to be published).

—

Georg Vrachliotis, *Geregelte Verhältnisse. Architektur und technisches Denken in der Epoche der Kybernetik,* Vienna, New York (forthcoming in 2010).

ILLUSTRATION CREDITS

Bschir

Fig. 1 Reprinted by permission from Macmillan Publishers Ltd: *Nature,* vol. 171, p. 737, copyright (1953).

Fig. 2 Reprinted by permission from Macmillan Publishers Ltd: *Nature,* vol. 173, p. 318, copyright (1954).

Dreyer

Fig. 1 Source: Charles Jencks and George Baird, *Meaning in Architecture,* New York, 1970, p. 143.

Fig. 2 © Heinrich Klotz, source: Heinrich Klotz: *Moderne und Postmoderne. Architektur der Gegenwart 1960–1980,* Braunschweig, Wiesbaden, 1984, p. 136.

Fig. 3 Source: Charles Jencks, *Towards a Symbolic Architecture. The Thematic House,* New York, 1985, p. 130.

Fig. 4 Source: Wolfgang Amsoneit, *Contemporary European Architects,* vol. 1, n. l., 1991, p. 89.

Fig. 5 © Andrea Gleiniger.

Fig. 6 Florathexplora (Toronto), flickr.com, creative commons.

Fig. 7 Torcello Trio (London), flickr.com, creative commons.

Vrachliotis

Fig. 1 Nicholas Negroponte, *The Architecture Machine,* Cambridge/Mass., 1970, p. 12.

Fig. 2 Nicholas Negroponte, *The Architecture Machine,* Cambridge/Mass., 1970, p. 18, 20 (sequence of images assembled by the author).

Fig. 3 © Frieder Nake, source: Jasia Reichardt (ed.), *Cybernetic Serendipity. The Computer and the Arts,* exhibition catalog, London, 1968, p. 77.

Fig. 4 © Georg Nees, source: Georg Nees, *Generative Computergraphik,* Erlangen, 1969, p. 241, 242.

Gleiniger

Fig. 1 © Heinrich Klotz, source: Heinrich Klotz, *Moderne und Postmoderne. Architektur der Gegenwart 1960–1980,* Braunschweig, Wiesbaden, 1984, p. 153.

Fig. 2 Philip Johnson, Mark Wigley, *Deconstructive Architecture,* exhibition catalog Museum of Modern Art New York, New York, London, 1988, p. 61.

Fig. 3 © ETH-Studio Monte Rosa/Toniatiuh Ambrosetti.

BIOGRAPHIES

—

Karim Bschir

is a research assistant at the Institute of Philosophy at ETH Zurich. After graduating from his studies in biochemistry at the University of Zurich, he completed a dissertation on philosophy. His main research interest is general scientific theory, particularly the question of scientific realism. Karim Bschir is also an affiliated researcher at the Collegium Helveticum and research fellow at the Center for Philosophy and the Natural Sciences (CPNS) at California State University, Sacramento.

—

Claus Dreyer

Studied philosophy and German studies, art history, and art education in Marburg, Berlin, and Stuttgart. Graduated in philosophy with the doctoral thesis *Semiotische Grundlagen der Architekturästhetik* (Semiotic foundations of architectural aesthetics), Stuttgart 1979. 1982–2009 professor for design foundations, spatial design, and design theory at the Department of Architecture and Interior Architecture at Ostwestfalen-Lippe University of Applied Sciences in Detmold. Numerous publications regarding in particular architecture and semiotics.

—

Andrea Gleiniger

Dr. phil., is a historian of art and architecture. Since 2007 she has been a lecturer at the Zurich University of the Arts, with a focus on the history and theory of space/scenography. She studied art history, comparative literature, and archaeology in Bonn and Marburg; in 1988, she took a doctorate in art history with a project on guiding ideas in large-scale postwar housing development; from 1983–93, she was curator at Deutsches Architekturmuseum Frankfurt/Main; since 1983, she has held teaching positions and guest professorships at academies in Karlsruhe, Stuttgart, and Zurich. From 2002–07, she was research assistant at the ETH Zurich/Chair of CAAD. She is active as a writer, particularly on architecture, urban planning, art, and new media in the 20th and 21st centuries.

—

Gabriele Gramelsberger

has been an academic assistant at the Institute for Philosophy at the Free University of Berlin since 2004. Studied philosophy, political science, and psychology in Berlin and Augsburg. Scholarship with the Department for Theory/Philosophy at the Jan van Eyck Academy, Maastricht. Doctorate in philosophy from the FU Berlin with a project in the philosophy of science, focusing on numerical simulation and visualization. Selected publication: Gabriele Gramelsberger (ed.), *From Science to Computational Sciences. Studies in the History of Computing and its Influence on Today's Science and Society*, Zurich, Berlin 2010.

—

Georg Trogemann

Since 1994 professor of experimental computer science at the Academy of Media Arts in Cologne. After completing his journeyman's examination in carpentry, studied computer science and mathematics at the University of Erlangen-Nürnberg. 1986–1990 worked as a research assistant at the University of Erlangen-Nürnberg on the SUPRENUM Project, a research endeavor aimed at developing a supercomputer for numerical applications. Graduated in 1990. Selected publication: *CodeArt – Eine elementare Einführung in die Programmierung als künstlerische Praktik*, Vienna, 2005.

—

Georg Vrachliotis

Academic assistant at the Institute for the History and Theory of Architecture at the ETH (Swiss Federal Institute of Technology) in Zurich, and guest lecturer in architectural theory at the Institute of Architectural Theory of Vienna University of Technology. Until 2009 served as academic assistant at the Chair for CAAD. He was visiting scholar at Freiburg and Bremen Universities and at the University of California at Berkeley and earned his doctorate in architecure 2009 from the ETH. His book *Geregelte Verhältnisse. Architektur und technisches Denken in der Epoche der Kybernetik* will be published by Springer Publishers in 2010.